Praise for Competing on Thought Leadership

"Thought leadership has been an important component in much of the value creation strategic advisory work I do within professional services. I've seen the approaches Bob puts forward in this book work time and time again — most recently in a human capital advisory firm that has grown 10X in value over the five years since Bob helped put in place a disciplined thought leadership strategy. In *Competing on Thought Leadership*, Bob walks you through each and every step. This book is a must-read for anyone looking to leverage the power of thought leadership in growing a professional services firm or any other growth-oriented organization."

—RICHARD ALDERSEA, Strategic Advisor to owners & operators
of professional services firms

"Bob nails the deep thinking and precision execution that separates leading thought leadership from also-rans. As he rightly notes, successful thought leadership starts with unique ideas that are substantiated through indisputable facts, figures and evidence, expressed through authentic experiences, and illuminated via compelling writing and design. The proof is in Bob's highly accessible frameworks that translate heady thought leadership concepts into achievable practice. Winning thought leadership initiatives aren't easy — nor are they for everyone. Success typically comes through iterative and egoless thinking, as well as a keen awareness of market wants, needs, desires, and zero tolerance for BS. Bob's practical guidebook puts the odds of success in the reader's favor. As such, it is truly a must-read for thought leadership practitioners and wannabes alike!"

—ALAN ALPER, Vice President, Global Thought Leadership Programs, Cognizant

"Finally, a marketing book that enables practical commercial execution. For those of us on the front line of sales, we are most grateful. *Competing on Thought Leadership* truly enables a unified commercial engine to connect marketing and sales with an executable solution so that, together, we can drive profitable revenue growth. This book brings sanity to the "more is better" barrage afflicting B2B buyers today and represents a powerful step to helping marketing and sales teams to mobilize together."

—MARIA BOULDEN, retired DuPont Global Sales Director,
"sales whisperer" to chief commercial officers worldwide

"Every chief marketing officer — and their bosses — need to adopt thought leadership as an integral part of their strategic plans. Companies must go beyond traditional marketing and learn how to lead on important societal issues. This book will show them how to do it."

—HANK CARDELLO, Senior Director, Leadership Solutions for Health &
Prosperity, Georgetown University McDonough School of Business

"Content matters! This practical book lays out clear, specific steps to achieve thought leadership and build a business on it."

—RAM CHARAN, global advisor to CEOs and bestselling author

"A must-read for any B2B business leaders competing for client mind share. It clearly lays out the steps that a business leader needs to take to go about setting a thought leadership strategy and then executing it. This book couldn't have been more timely. Businesses around the world are trying to understand how to engage with clients and prospects in meaningful conversations in the new world."

—BINAYAK CHOUDHURY, Co-Founder and Partner, Phronesis Partners (global research and analytics firm)

"*Competing on Thought Leadership* is a powerful guide for those determined to win with breakthrough thinking. Buday reminds us that it is a tight combination of demand creation (creating desire for the new idea) and supply creation (being able to deliver and scale the new idea) that ultimately creates a scalable solution. This is a must-have handbook for any leadership team competing on new ideas in today's age of disruption."

—SHANE CRAGUN, Senior Partner, Leadership Development, Korn Ferry, and co-author of *Reinvention: Accelerating Results in the Age of Disruption*

"Today's knowledge-intensive firms compete in a world where success accrues to those with the best ideas. But that's just one piece of the puzzle. As Bob Buday tells us in this insightful book, thought leadership has its own distinctive value chain, demanding focus from idea generation all the way through to providing expertise at scale. He has a distinguished career in helping companies achieve success as thought leaders. As the director of a university think tank, I found the advice in the book to be extremely valuable."

—VIJAY GURBAXANI, Director of the Center for Digital Transformation, University of California, Irvine, Paul Merage School of Business

"Outstanding speechwriters 'reach for the marble.' They frame bold ideas that are so compelling and elegant that they are worthy of being carved into stone and memorialized for future generations. But it is not just speechwriters. Most leaders in the private, public and civic sectors harbor this dream. As they lead with thoughts, they hope to forever etch their core beliefs and insights into the minds of the people they are aiming to inspire and influence. In *Competing on Thought Leadership*, readers receive a master class in transforming this dream into a reality. If you aspire to positively change the world with your ideas, you owe it to yourself to read this book!"

—MARK LEITER, Chairman, Leiter & Company, Former Chief Strategy Officer of Nielsen, Former McKinsey & Co. B2B marketing practice co-leader

"Every company that's trying to create disruptive change in the marketplace needs to be seen as a thought leader today. Thought leaders are crucial to getting an audience to see and solve their problems in a very different way. Thought leaders ignite that change. Robert Buday shows you step-by-step exactly how to make thought leadership a winning business strategy."

—CHARLENE LI, *New York Times* bestselling author of *The Disruption Mindset* and Founder of Altimeter

"Read one chapter and you'll move ahead of your competition; read them all and you'll own them. Bob Buday not only defines thought leadership, he simplifies it, and then he delivers it."

—JEFF MCKAY, CEO of Prudent Pedal and B2B Marketing Strategist

"Thought leadership isn't a new idea, but what's new about this book is that Buday does a marvelous job of taking thought leadership from something resembling voodoo to nearly a hard science. In so doing, he provides an end-to-end playbook for how to monetize it and grow a business around it. Filled with rich examples of what and what not to do, this is a great read."

—RIC MERRIFIELD, Author of *Rethink and Surviving a Business Earthquake,* and co-author of the classic *Harvard Business Review* article, "The Next Revolution in Productivity."

"The definitive book on thought leadership from the world's most knowledgeable expert on the topic, *Competing on Thought Leadership* is as educational as it is useful. Bob Buday combines his keen insight on why thought leadership is exploding in popularity with his well-earned life wisdom on how to develop compelling content and turn it into rapid growth in revenue and profit. This book is a must-read for executives in every organization that compete on expertise, ideas, and insight."

—JASON MLICKI, Principal, Rattleback

"Thought leadership is the engine that drives the early adoption of disruptive innovations. It inspires visionary customers not only to embrace a new paradigm but to set aside budget to incorporate it into their future plans. *Competing on Thought Leadership* is an essential guide to navigating this challenging terrain."

—GEOFFREY MOORE, Author, *Crossing the Chasm* and *Zone to Win*

"This book provides ample evidence to what many of us already knew: Bob Buday is a thought leader on thought leadership. There should be no doubt that our current disruptive times already place us in the 'Golden Age for Thought Leadership' that Bob describes so well. Remember, however, that 'Golden Ages' always translate into outsized rewards for a few winners and enormous challenges for the many displaced market leaders, also-rans and downright losers. In this book, Bob distills his decades hard-earned lessons into a thoughtful approach that could increase your odds of being among the winners, rather than swimming with the losers. Ignore it at your own peril!"

—CHUNKA MUI, author, *A Brief History of a Perfect Future: Inventing the World We Can Proudly Leave Our Kids by 2050,* and Founding Partner, Future Histories Group

"Thought leadership is no longer just for marketing but can be a powerful way to guide competitive strategy. Buday offers the ultimate pro's guide, so that companies can take the next logical step: toward developing insights so enduring that they can give you a long-term edge in creating new services for customers."

—EVAN I. SCHWARTZ, former Director of Storytelling, Innosight

"This book provides invaluable vision for and lessons in thought leadership. I especially appreciate the framework for how visual communications, data visualization, and interactive experiences fit into the field. I cut my teeth doing this work for the thought leadership departments at many of the white shoe and Big Four consulting firms I greatly value Bob's insights into how to best take advantage of these technologies and methods in the context of thought leadership."

—BILL SHANDER, CEO and Founder of Beehive Media, expert on information design, data storytelling and visualization

"This book shows companies and experts that have mastered their subject how to powerfully attract more and more work. Midsized companies should use this approach to leap ahead of their bigger competition. Buday is the thought leadership master of today for any leading thinker who can walk their talk. We followed his methods and grew our consulting firm revenues 4X. If you think of yourself or your firm as a thought leader, read this book now."

—ROBERT SHER, CEO of Mastering Midsized, Author of *Mighty Midsized Companies* and *Driving Midsized Growth: People*

"Bob Buday was one of the inventors of thought leadership for professional services firms — a master practitioner — who since then has taught what he knows and is still learning — a master instructor. This is a very smart book. It gives practical advice about how to use thought leadership to compete, and it is as clear-eyed about how things go wrong as it is sharp-eyed about how to succeed."

—THOMAS A. STEWART, Chief Knowledge Officer, AchieveNEXT and former Editor in Chief, *Harvard Business Review*

"Bob is clearly the thought leader on thought leadership. He captures the keys to 'ideas with impact' with creative insights, specific steps, and relevant examples. Any leader who recognizes the value of ideas will cherish this blueprint for action. Following Bob's guidelines will make knowledge productive."

—DAVE ULRICH, Rensis Likert Professor, Ross School of Business, University of Michigan Partner, The RBL Group

"Bob Buday has been the wise sage behind thought leadership and strategic initiatives for countless companies. Working behind the scenes, he has skillfully crafted new, out-of-the box direction for companies. He has also helped them clarify their messages and get published in high-profile publications such as *Harvard Business Review*. Now after decades of being the guru behind the scenes, Buday has generously documented his knowledge on thought leadership in this compelling book. Leadership of companies desiring to remain competitive and relevant should feel compelled to take note!"

—JAMES C. WETHERBE, Richard Schulze Distinguished Professor of Business, Texas Tech University

COMPETING ON THOUGHT LEADERSHIP

COMPETING

ON

THOUGHT

LEADERSHIP

HOW GREAT B2B COMPANIES
TURN EXPERTISE INTO REVENUE

ROBERT S. BUDAY

IDEAPRESS
PUBLISHING

WASHINGTON, D.C.

IDEAPRESS
PUBLISHING

Printed in the United States.

Ideapress Publishing | www.ideapresspublishing.com

Cover Design: Lindy Martin, Faceout Studios
Interior Design: Jessica Angerstein

Cataloging-in-Publication Data is on file with the Library of Congress.

ISBN: 978-1-64687-100-1

Special Sales
Ideapress Books are available at a special discount for bulk purchases for sales promotions and premiums, or for use in corporate training programs. Special editions, including personalized covers, a custom foreword, corporate imprints, and bonus content are also available.

For the greatest loves of my life —
Cathy and our precious children: Rachel M.,
Jesse, Rachel F., Benjamin, Ryan, and John.

And for aspiring thought leaders who aim
to make a big, beneficial impact on the world,
and the people who help them do it.

CONTENTS

Part VI: Turbocharging Thought Leadership

LIFE AT THE EPICENTER OF A BLOCKBUSTER CONCEPT

+   +   +   +   +   +   +   +

I N THE SUMMER OF 1993, CSC Index was riding high. The consulting firm was a supernova propelled by a blockbuster concept that companies everywhere were embracing: business reengineering. The idea was about harnessing information technology to redesign workflows and processes for massive improvements in costs, time to market and quality. Big, blue-chip companies — Bell Atlantic (which later became part of Verizon), Hallmark Cards, Amoco, Viacom, Pepsi, Lloyds Bank and dozens of other CSC Index clients — were zealously reengineering their businesses.

Index was the shining star of the consulting industry. With its charismatic research partner and godfather of reengineering Michael

Hammer riding alongside it, the Cambridge, Massachusetts-based company had quadrupled its revenue in five years, to $150 million.

I was part of the marketing team that helped bring reengineering and Index to the cover of *Fortune* and other prestigious publications. It was an exhilarating time at an exhilarating place, pulsating with the energy of smart, creative people with strong ideas, and clients waiting in line to be "reengineered."

Seven years later, CSC Index was out of business. The shining star had become a shooting star, falling back to earth, but with a whimper.

What happened? My postmortem (and it's not the only one) is simple: CSC Index lived and died by the sword of thought leadership.

When CSC Index was living by the sword, it was a wonderful place to be a marketer, to run its publications and PR activities. In fact, in the summer of 1993 I felt the company was about to explode, and in the positive use of the term. The firm and Hammer had brought reengineering to the business world three years earlier. I could just sense it would become a blockbuster. And while the consulting sector is certainly not as sexy as, say, the movie industry, reengineering did become management consulting's blockbuster hit that year, and for several years afterward. In fact, the prominent research firm Gartner Inc. sized the global market for reengineering consulting services in 1995 at $4.7 billion.[1]

I believed that the firm, whose Cambridge office I commuted to nearly every weekday for 10 years, was about to rocket higher that year. How did I know? We had just hit the trifecta in "thought leadership": a mega-bestselling business book (*Reengineering the Corporation* was on *The New York Times* list of *general* books for 41 weeks);[2] a cover story in a prominent business publication (*Fortune*) on the global trend the firm had created;[3] and, three years earlier, a classic article in the world's most prestigious management publication (*Harvard Business Review*).[4]

Yet I was supremely confident about CSC Index's near-term future for a more important reason. I knew its pioneering reengineering service had produced outsized results for several clients. As every marketer hopes about the efficacy of the products they are promoting, this was a big relief for me, and a source of pride in the company I was working for. Consulting firms were known to over-promise and under-deliver. Their claims of expertise in the books and articles they wrote often did not square with reality.

In contrast, CSC Index's reputation with reengineering in its early days of the service was stellar. It enabled Bell Atlantic to cut the time it took to execute a key revenue-generating process from 16 days to just hours. It reduced Hallmark Cards' new product development cycle substantially.

By 1995, Index's revenue had grown even more, to $200 million, five times the revenue of the firm when I went to work for it in 1987. But in the second half of the 1990s, Index began dying by the sword of thought leadership. And it wasn't a pretty death.

THE DEATH OF CSC INDEX

The exits of key people didn't help. Hammer ended his research partnership with the firm in 1994,[5] and Jim Champy, the CEO who steered CSC Index to its rapid growth, left in 1996.[6] Neither did reports alleging Index manipulated one of its books onto bestseller lists.[7]

Still, I argue that the firm's biggest failings were on the supply side of thought leadership. Other, and much bigger, consulting firms like Deloitte and Andersen Consulting (later rebranded as Accenture) created their own versions of reengineering. With more rigorous and extensive internal training and methodology development programs, these firms and their professionals were ready to meet the demand that the reengineering craze had unleashed. CSC Index, the company that launched the craze, was not ready for the deluge that followed. Ultimately, competitors proved to be a more reliable choice — even if they weren't the innovators.

The story of CSC Index is but one of many in the annals of thought leadership. Their lessons show that inventing revolutionary concepts that improve how businesses operate, marketing those concepts well, and attracting adulation and new business are not enough. Companies that wish to compete on the basis of having superior expertise — to compete on thought leadership — must do more. They have to be able to deliver that expertise at scale when a groundswell of clients shows up and asks for it. This is where CSC Index fell short.

Nonetheless, CSC Index was a pioneer in *the practice of thought leadership*, not just in the development of the business reengineering concept. To be sure, other consulting firms for years had programs to capture and disseminate their expertise. For example, McKinsey and Boston Consulting Group regularly began publishing thought leadership journals in the 1960s. But few consulting firms had an R&D think tank of the type that CSC Index and Mike Hammer built, an extensive conference business that wined and dined prospects at top resorts, and publications, book publishing and public relations programs that got its consultants' writings on clients' desks.

CSC Index showed consulting firms everywhere what thought leadership could do for them. Ever since, the practice has become wildly popular, broadly adopted but still misunderstood and too loosely interpreted — within and far outside the consulting industry. The label "thought leadership" is slapped on blog posts, white papers, research reports, sections of websites and many other things that turn out to be (upon inspection) not highly thoughtful.

Many professional services firms might become enamored of the idea of being regarded as thought leaders. Some, in fact, get very good at developing big ideas, and even better at marketing them. But that's all they get good at. They are still failing to adopt all of the practices that underpin genuine thought leadership and help them turn it into revenue — from the research-driven data that supports the big idea, to the marketing that showcases it to influencers and potential clients, to the capability improvements that enable the company to meet the surge in demand for its services.

This book will explore these dimensions of thought leadership. We'll examine how companies can generate demand for *and* supply of their expertise, so they don't turn into shooting stars that fade away. If you lead a professional services or other B2B firm, or serve as a C-suite executive at one, or if you are a consultant or a research or marketing specialist in these sectors, this book is for you.

Over the next few chapters, we'll look at the historical evolution of thought leadership and how the processes of developing and marketing it have evolved over time. We will introduce a number of frameworks that explain how to achieve recognition and revenue from thought leadership, including:

- The four pillars of competing on thought leadership: a highly focused topic strategy; case study-based content R&D; a low-bias, high-bandwidth marketing and sales mix; and methodology, internal training and recruiting that can scale the delivery of exceptional services.

- The nine hallmarks of excellence for the best thought leadership content.

- The six elements of a persuasive argument — the problem/ solution outline template.

- The "ripples in a pond" approach to help breakthrough ideas spread far and wide.

Other chapters of this book delve deeply into how original research and a company's field experience can shape powerful arguments and successful solutions to business problems; how to use data visualization and other powerful tools to generate excitement and interest on your company's website; and how the best companies get buy-in from their leaders to compete on the basis of thought leadership.

After more than three decades in the thought leadership marketing profession, I've seen the CSC Index story — of B2B firms codifying, creating demand for and generating supply of big ideas for improving other businesses — play itself out time and again. There have been other precedent-setting concepts: customer loyalty management, disruptive innovation, blue ocean strategy, lean startup, and emotional intelligence, to name just a few. And along with these standout concepts, a lot of useless debris calling itself thought leadership is now floating around in the vast cosmos of business ideas. The quest for thought leadership has become a crowded stage.

But I need to pause here because I've loosely thrown around the term — thought leadership — that's central to this book. To follow my thinking on this subject requires understanding my definition of it. There are many other definitions out there, most of which only discuss demand-creation pieces of the elephant. The next chapter explores the whole beast.

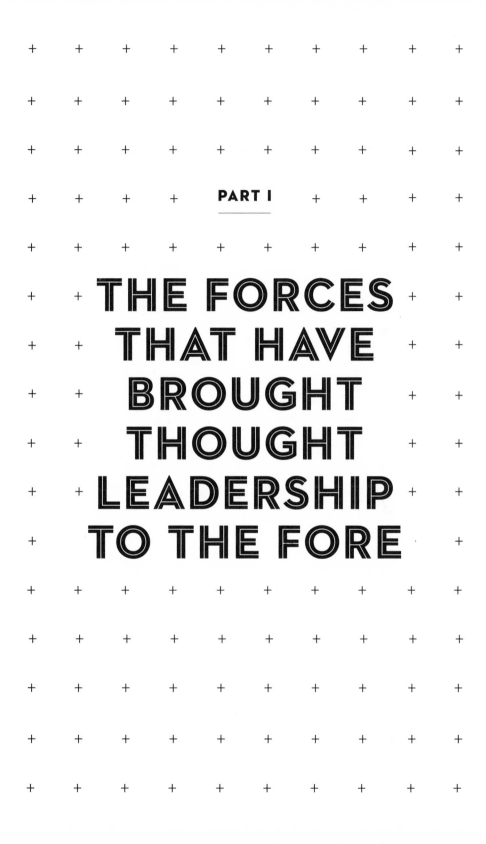

PART I

THE FORCES THAT HAVE BROUGHT THOUGHT LEADERSHIP TO THE FORE

CHAPTER 1

A MORE ENCOMPASSING DEFINITION OF THOUGHT LEADERSHIP

+ + + + + + + +

THE WORDS "THOUGHT LEADERSHIP" have become part of the corporate lexicon. They seem to appear in just about every business-to-business company website (e.g., "Insights" sections that dispense organizational wisdom). They pop up in numerous job postings (e.g., "Global Head of Thought Leadership"). They can be found in many PR plans (e.g., "Make the CEO a recognized thought leader on XYZ"). And they are slapped as a label on seemingly every white paper, conference presentation and other documents to make their ideas appear more novel and substantive than they perhaps are.

It seems every B2B company these days, and especially the ones that sell expertise by the hour, wants to be viewed as a "thought leader." And so do many software, financial services and other companies that want to demonstrate the expertise of the people who produce and deliver those offerings. In fact, fortunes have been made by professional services firms that turned their expertise into world-recognized concepts.

Yet the chances for a B2B company's "thoughts" to become blockbuster ideas are slim. The competition for executive mindshare is ferocious. Google and social media make it easy for executives to find content on just about every topic, and for companies to spread their ideas.

Moreover, the easy availability of digital tools for spreading ideas and building your brand has created a deafening marketplace of ideas, where it's easy for fast-buck peddlers to pretend to be something that they're not. The sheer number of authoritative-sounding websites that include "thought leadership" make it difficult for B2B companies that need real solutions to identify those that are truly proven and effective. And perhaps the most troubling aspect of the thought leadership profession today is that even when a firm can offer proven ideas, it may not have the capacity to deliver when potential clients find them.

So let's cut through the clutter by defining what thought leadership really is:

Thought leadership is *the acclaim that an organization or individual achieves by becoming known for providing superior expertise that solves a complex problem.*

Thought leaders are people and the organizations they work for that develop, deliver, market and sell solutions (advice, training, software and other offerings) that are better at solving certain problems of people, organizations and the greater society. Firms that gain substantial and sustainable market advantages with thought leadership excel in four areas:

1. **They focus their thought leadership resources on building deep and superior expertise on a small number of client problems.** Of course, the bigger the firm, the greater the number of client problems it can focus on; the smaller the firm, the fewer. Deciding which client problems to focus on is at the core of an effective thought leadership strategy.

2. **They create groundbreaking ideas about how to solve the client problems they've decided to "own."** A key way they create such ideas is by conducting primary research and collecting key lessons from their client projects. They create content that codifies the superior ways they solve client problems, based on this research and client experience. These activities are, in effect, their thought leadership research and development engine.

3. **They turn their thought leadership R&D content into material that becomes a wellspring for marketing and sales campaigns:** books, research reports, op-ed submissions, conference presentations, etc.

4. **They also turn their thought leadership content into methodologies and internal training curricula.** By doing so, they increase the number of people in their firms who can deliver this expertise to clients at a high level of quality.

THE 4 PILLARS OF THOUGHT LEADERSHIP

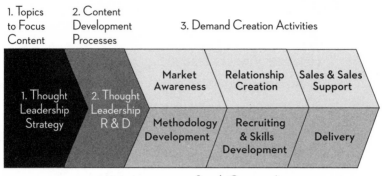

1. Topics to Focus Content   2. Content Development Processes   3. Demand Creation Activities

1. Thought Leadership Strategy   2. Thought Leadership R & D

Market Awareness   Relationship Creation   Sales & Sales Support

Methodology Development   Recruiting & Skills Development   Delivery

4. Supply Creation Activities

As you can see, marketing and sales (i.e., demand creation) are just one of the four pillars — albeit an important one. But if you've read the more than 30 books on thought leadership over the last 20 years, you'd think it was the only one. It isn't, and it can't be — not if your firm wants to outpace competitors by providing expertise that is superior at solving your customers' problems.

This is a broader definition of thought leadership. Companies that adopt it recognize that they are *competing* on the basis of thought leadership — not just *marketing* on that basis.

Defined this way, CSC Index was squarely competing on the basis of thought leadership. But it didn't take the supply-creation piece nearly as seriously as the demand-generation piece.

Since the turn of the 21st century, many other firms have begun to take notice of how consulting firms used thought leadership to expand their businesses. The practice of thought leadership has been adopted and embraced by companies in the software, wealth management, law, architecture and accounting industries, among others.

The race to be recognized as a preeminent expert has been in full swing. And like business reengineering, a number of blockbuster concepts have had their moments: Clayton Christensen's concept of "disruptive innovation" (followed by Silicon Valley startups and their financiers, which have transformed the media, retail, transportation, advertising and other sectors); Bain & Company's customer loyalty and Net Promoter Score consulting services (forcing companies to root out poor service); various quality improvement methods (Six Sigma, TQM, etc.); and the lean startup, to name just a few.

Each concept helped organizations that adopted them improve their businesses, often substantially. And, of course, they have enabled the producers of the concepts to grow their own businesses.

What is of little doubt is that the concept behind these concepts — of competing on the basis of thought leadership — has gained substantial traction since the 1990s. How do I know this? I see five telltale signs:

- The explosion of books that use the phrase "thought leadership."

- The ascension of conferences designed purely to feature thought leaders, and only thought leaders.

- The deluge of blog posts by both accomplished people and dilettantes opining on seemingly every topic under the sun.

- The rise of B2B companies that aren't in the publishing business to publish thought leadership periodicals.

- The hundreds of thousands of people around the world with thought leadership in their job titles or job descriptions.

Let's explore each one.

THE 21ST CENTURY THOUGHT LEADERSHIP GOLD RUSH

There's nothing magical about the year 2000. The 20-year uptake of thought leadership practices outside the management consulting industry began before then. But it gained steam after the turn of the century. A number of indicators, the first of which has to do with books, tells us this.

Book Authors Embrace the Phrase

One indicator is a statistic that Google compiles: its Ngram Viewer. This is a measure, year by year, of how many times a term shows up in the millions of books that Google has digitally catalogued since 2004. Some of those books were published hundreds of years ago.

You didn't know that Google scanned books in addition to websites? Eight years after three Stanford University students (including Google founders Larry Page and Sergey Brin) began building a tool to help web searchers find information, the company began scanning books. By then, Google had become the dominant search engine and a hugely profitable company. (Since 2004, its revenue has grown from $3 billion to $182 billion, and its profits have soared from about $400 million to $34 billion.[8])

By 2015, the company had scanned 20 million books, the contents of which can be found with a few simple clicks of a keyboard.[9] With those books in digital form, it's possible for Google's high-powered computers and software to find words and phrases rapidly. That enables you to see the rise or fall of trends, as captured in books.

Google's Ngram Viewer is nearly current. As the company explains in a web page about it, you can type in "child care" and see that the phrase took off in books published in the late 1960s, but that it has been declining since 1990.[10]

What about the trend of "thought leadership," as mentioned in books in the last 50 years? Growth in the usage of the phrase was flat from 1970 to 1990, and then soared between 1990 and 2008. Since then, its appearance in books has continued to rise, although at a slower pace.

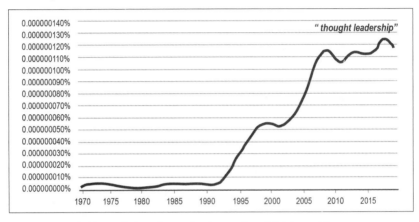

The Rise of Thought Leadership on Google's Ngram Viewer

Another metric showing the hunger for thought leadership can be found in the market for self-help books. This category is one I can directly associate with my definition of thought leadership — people who gain renown by providing advice to solve problems. In the U.S., the number of self-help books sold almost doubled between 2011 and 2019, to 18.6 million. The number of self-help book titles nearly tripled in that time, from 31,000 to 85,000.[11]

One more book metric of the insatiable appetite for thought leadership is the number of books written on the topic itself. In an Amazon search, I counted more than 30 at the time I wrote this book. (That includes one that I and three co-authors published in 2008.[12])

The Rise of Two Conferences for Thought Leaders: Davos and TED

Another telling statistic is the number of speaking events showcasing aspiring or already recognized thought leaders. For sure, experts have been speaking at business and industry conferences for decades. Conferences have always been an outlet for thought leaders. But they haven't been the focal point. Before thought leadership became a popular trend in the 1990s, these experts have shared the stage with other speakers who presented their companies' experiences. Thought leaders speaking at conferences also shared the conference grounds with conference booths hawking products and services. In other words, hearing a thought leader present at an industry conference was just a small part of the show — especially when the speaker was of the motivational type.

But until late in the 20th century, few conferences were designed purely around presentations — thoughtful content. But that began to change in the mid-1980s. Since then, two now-immensely popular events — the World Economic Forum's annual conference in Davos and the now-ubiquitous TED Talks — have taken center stage as pure thought leadership events. They have shown that thought leaders can gain big audiences without the other accoutrements of business conferences. They also signify that thought leadership is highly coveted.

Let's start with the WEF. In 1971, Klaus Schwab, a business policy professor at the University of Geneva, Switzerland, created the European Management Forum in Geneva. His initial concept was gathering European business leaders for an annual meeting in the Swiss resort village of Davos to discuss management practices from U.S. companies. By 1987, Schwab renamed his group the World Economic Forum to reflect its global attendance and perspective. Every year in

January, the ever-expanding group meets for a week in the village to hear presentations and attend networking and social events.[13]

Just before the pandemic's onset, the Davos 2020 event alone attracted nearly 3,000 attendees from more than 100 nations.[14] They included country leaders (e.g., Donald Trump and Angela Merkel). The WEF says its members number 1,000 companies today, and they include many of the Fortune 500: AstraZeneca, Walmart, WPP, Amazon, Adobe, AT&T, Procter & Gamble, PwC and PepsiCo, to name just a few. Given the audience and the event's prestige, speaking at Davos is an honor, and 600 speakers present each year. It's a thought leader's paradise.

TED's rise was similarly meteoric, but it didn't move into full throttle until two decades after Klaus Schwab launched his predecessor to the WEF. TED stands for Technology, Entertainment and Design, and those were the three fields that TED co-founders Richard Saul Wurman and Harry Marks wanted to merge in a conference when they staged their first TED event back in February 1984 in Monterey, California. Wurman was an architect, graphic designer and author; Marks was a broadcast design artist. They attracted 300 people to the event, including Apple co-founder Steve Jobs (although he didn't present). Half the audience paid nothing, as Wurman tried to fill seats.[15] But the event lost money,[16] and the founders put their idea on ice for six years.

Fortunately, they didn't give up. In 1990 — perhaps more than coincidentally, the time in which thought leadership was taking off beyond the consulting world — Wurman and Marks relaunched the conference. It turned a profit this time, and it would soon become an annual success. By 1992, the event was inviting and charging a thousand people $4,000 each or more to listen to 18-minute presentations.[17]

Speakers included the founders of Google (Larry Page and Sergey Brin), actor Michael Douglas and musician Herbie Hancock.[18]

In 2001, Wurman sold TED to the former editor of *Wired* magazine, Chris Anderson, who moved the event 340 miles down the California coast to Long Beach. It's become even more popular under his leadership. Anderson proceeded to launch a sister conference (TEDGlobal) and line extensions from them: one for women, one for middle and high school students, and smaller, independently run city events (dubbed "TEDx"). He also decided there was a big online audience for the best TED talks. In 2006, Anderson began posting archived TED talks and by 2009 the number of views of those and other presentations had reached 100 million. That number had increased 10-fold three years later.[19]

By 2019, the TED Talk channel had featured 4,000 videos, and the independent TEDx events had posted almost 140,000 videos.[20] By 2017, Anderson was sitting on a $65 million business, charging $8,500 per seat.[21] It's a place for thought leaders who want global impact.

Long after co-founders Wurman (86 years old and alive as of this writing) and Marks (who died at 88 in 2019) departed from TED, the concept has blossomed perhaps beyond their wildest dreams. For thought leaders around the world, Davos and TED have provided global, highly regarded outlets for their ideas.

The Explosion of Thought Leadership Articles on the Web

The trend statistics on books mentioning and being devoted to thought leadership, and the ascension of conferences like TED and the WEF, are not the only signposts of thought leadership's ascension. The many publications and articles written by people hoping to establish their expertise are another sign of fervent interest.

Blogs are one of them. The term "blog" comes from the slightly longer term "weblog." The term "blog" was supposedly coined by Jorn Barger (an American who started a website called Robot Wisdom in 1995).[22] "Weblog" is credited to Peter Merholz. It's no secret that blogging has exploded since the World Wide Web's ascension in the 1990s. Nearly a third of the 1.7 billion websites on the internet have blogs — 600 million, in fact. They produced more than two billion blog posts in 2018.[23]

Are all these blog posts written by topic experts, or people knowledgeable about topics and trying to become recognized as experts? Of course not. Nonetheless, one can assume that millions of bloggers *are* trying to demonstrate their expertise to the entire world.

The Surge in New B2B Publishers

Businesses for many years have been well-supported by a publishing industry serving up news on competitors and regulations, and advice on running their enterprises. Business publications that cross industries — *The Wall Street Journal, Fortune, Forbes, Bloomberg Businessweek,* among the biggest, and more recently digital upstarts such as *Business Insider* and *Axios* — have been staples of executive readers. So have business school journals such as *Harvard Business Review, MIT Sloan Management Review, Knowledge@Wharton* and dozens of others in narrow academic niches.

Yet many B2B companies that sell expertise have decided they needed their own versions of these journals to ensure their ideas are heard. In the management consulting industry, McKinsey (*McKinsey Quarterly* in 1964) and Boston Consulting Group (*BCG Perspectives* in 1964) have had thought leadership journals since the 1960s. Others are more relative newcomers: Booz Allen (now part of PwC, launching *Strategy + Business* in 1995), Roland Berger (*Think:Act* in 2004),

Cognizant (*Cognizanti Journal* in 2007), Tata Consultancy Services (*Perspectives* in 2009) and Deloitte (*Deloitte Review* in 2007) among them. So have multibillion-dollar software companies like SAP (*Digitalist*, from 2015 to 2020), Oracle (*Profit*, since 1995) and ServiceNow (*Workflow Quarterly*, since 2018).

Other B2B firms such as venture capital powerhouse Andreessen Horowitz (an investor in Facebook, Zynga, Lyft, Slack, Pinterest and other startup successes) don't have branded thought leadership journals. Nonetheless, their websites publish dozens of articles and other content, alongside the traditional sections of a website.

Why do such VCs want to be regarded as thought leaders? Andreessen Horowitz wants to influence its audience of entrepreneurs and investors without having a media interpreter in the middle. As Margit Wennmachers, operating partner at the firm, blogged on the firm's website, "We embraced speaking directly to our audience — from the builders of the future to the tech-curious — right as the firm was started in 2009." It began with blogs about why the firm funded certain founders. The VC's blogging later opined on technologies and practices in helping entrepreneurs scale firms. "Having this direct channel to express our thinking was powerful. Entrepreneurs felt that we 'got' them, their tech, and their industries. Big companies found it was useful to learn about the new technologies and trends, as well as how these newfangled modern companies were being built."[24]

This venture capital firm, known as "a16z" for short (because 16 letters in the alphabet stand between the A in Andreessen and the Z of Horowitz),[25] has since expanded its thought leadership content into podcasts and books.

It's hard to find statistics on how many B2B companies that *aren't* in the publishing business are publishing thought leadership journals. But data from the popular web content management system firm WordPress provides some clues. In 2018, about two-thirds of its new business customers were media publishing companies and about a third were corporate marketers (the non-publisher publishers). By 2020, that ratio had nearly flipped. Some 62 percent of new customers were corporate marketers and only 38 percent of them were publishers.[26]

Lots of Thought Leaders, and People Helping Them

Perhaps the most telling sign that a profession is emerging, or has indeed arrived, is the number of people who make a living from it. On this count, the numbers are fascinating, and they come from LinkedIn, the social network for people who work for organizations or themselves.

You no doubt know about and use LinkedIn. Its growth has been meteoric. At the start of 2021, LinkedIn boasted of having more than 700 million members in over 200 countries. That included 55 million companies.[27]

I use the LinkedIn statistic to show how many people are involved in some manner in thought leadership — even if it's just a small part of their job. LinkedIn has 496,000 people who have "thought leadership" in their job titles or descriptions. That's based on a search I did in September 2021. Some work in top levels of their company — ranging from a senior vice president of thought leadership at Fidelity Investments (the $20 billion revenue investment firm[28]), a VP of thought leadership at the $13 billion automotive supplier Aptiv,[29] and a VP of content and thought leadership at business data supplier IRI. Even music industry pioneer Spotify has a global lead for thought leadership research. She's been in that role for more than four years.

Imagine that: Nearly 500,000 people around the world are involved in thought leadership.

There's no question that thought leadership has become a white-hot field. The signposts are everywhere. The question might be, *why*? Why are so many people and so many companies in B2B sectors trying to communicate their expertise in articles, speeches, seminars, webinars, blog posts, books and their own *Harvard Business Review*-looking company management journals?

That's the question I address in the next chapter.

CHAPTER 2

WHY ARE COMPANIES HUNGRY FOR THOUGHT LEADERSHIP?

+ + + + + + + +

I HOPE THE PREVIOUS CHAPTER convinced you, if you weren't convinced already, that the demand for thought leaders — and for people to help them become thought leaders — has grown inexorably over the last three decades.

This chapter is my take on what's behind the trend. Why has there been a spike since the early 1990s in the usage of the term "thought leadership" in books? Why have an increasing number of executives, managers and the non-managerial public been flocking to business conferences devoted solely to hearing experts impart their expertise?

What explains the mushrooming number of blogs written by people to show off their smarts — and the exponential growth in their readership?

Why, when so many print publications have been disappearing as Google and Facebook sucked the advertising lifeblood from their veins, have so many B2B companies that *don't* publish for a living become publishers of thought leadership content?

In my view, it boils down to a world of escalating complexity. Executives need to figure out their companies' strategic direction, how to create demand and supply for their products and services, how to stage productive innovation, and how to attract and keep talented people. These and many more issues have become increasingly difficult to sort out.

Mounting complexity in running companies such as those that I've mentioned — especially large ones with many moving parts (customer segments, suppliers, employees, etc.) in many markets around the world — is fueling the demand for, and the supply of, deep and specialized expertise. Individuals and whole firms with superior expertise, *and* that are highly skilled at letting their audiences know about it, become known as thought leaders.

In this chapter, I'll look at what I believe are the biggest factors behind such rising business complexity. I'll then show how the forces of complexity have been at work — in decreasing the half-lives of companies, the jobs of top executives and even the fortunes of entire sectors.

Finally, I'll explain why certain companies have gained an edge in getting in the door of customers whose businesses are being wrenched by rising complexity. The short answer is that when there are many suppliers of services and products that can answer a company's complex problems, the suppliers that create coherence out of the chaos are the ones that get invited in to solve those problems.

SIGNS OF A MORE BRUTAL GLOBAL ECONOMY

Life in running companies has become more difficult, even treacherous for some, over these past three decades. While many factors explain why, I believe four are the most telling:

- **The shrinking time in which the biggest companies stay the biggest.** According to an analysis of the S&P 500 list of 1964, the average firm had been on the list for 33 years. By 2016, the rate fell to 24 years. By 2027, the rate is predicted to be 12 years — half the average tenure just 11 years earlier.[30] Bragging rights for being among the 500 biggest American companies, year after year, will be harder to earn.

- **Faster turnover of CEOs and other executives in big companies.** Another study tracked CEO entrances and exits since 2000 at the world's 2,500 biggest publicly held companies; it found the annual turnover rate grew from 12.9 percent in 2000 to 17.5 percent in 2018.[31] CEOs aren't the only members of the C-suite with less job security. In the U.S., chief marketing officers at the biggest advertisers have also been having shorter stays in the same role since 2014, according to recruiter Spencer Stuart. In that year, the average tenure for a CMO was 48 months. It fell to 44 months the next year, and to 42 months in 2016, and 41 months in 2019.[32]

- **The accelerating rise and fall of entire sectors.** Industries (many of them born out of the internet) that weren't around

30 years ago are flourishing, and others that have been here for centuries appear to be dying. The newspaper industry is the poster child for internet-induced destruction. Revenue of U.S. newspapers plummeted 71 percent, from $49 billion in 2005 to $14 billion in 2018.[33] The pandemic of 2020-2021 accelerated the carnage; a Pew Research study of 300 newspapers showed that advertising revenue fell by 42 percent from 2019 to 2020.[34] Whose fortunes have been rising? One of them is the digital industry — the companies that sell computer and communications hardware, software and support services to put that technology to use in organizations. This sector represented 7.3 percent of U.S. GDP in 2005. By 2018, its revenue had doubled (to $1.8 trillion), and its share of GDP had grown to 9.0 percent.[35,36] In fact, the digital sector is now larger than financial services and insurance.

- **The dominance of intangible over tangible corporate assets.** Just 50 years ago, tangible assets such as real estate, factories, buildings, equipment and stock in inventory far overshadowed intangible assets (patents on processes and designs, brand value, data, software, etc.) on corporate balance sheets. That situation has completely reversed itself since 1975, when 83 percent of S&P 500 company assets were tangible. In 2020, only 10 percent of assets were tangible, while *90 percent* were intangible.[37] I argue that the high "intangibility" of business has made it much harder for executives to understand what to do, and what others are doing. It's easier to understand what your competitors are doing when you can see the result of their strategies — the way a retailer organizes its stores or where a manufacturer locates plants.

Walmart founder Sam Walton was known to troll the aisles of rival stores to make sure his prices were competitive.[38] But competitors' intangible assets are harder to untangle.

These four factors — shrinking corporate half-lives, shorter executive tenures, the emergence and disappearance of whole industries and the shift from tangible to intangible assets — all speak to how difficult it has become for big companies to stay vibrant. Their leaders are dealing with greater complexities, and many have been turning to thought leaders to sort them out.

FORCES OF COMPLEXITY THAT HAVE INCREASED DEMAND FOR BUSINESS EXPERTISE

Numerous factors have shortened the shelf lives of companies in the last 30 years. I'm going to focus on three of the biggest complexities that *my* clients in the last 30 years have seen in *their* clients:

- Growing customer sophistication, expansion and fragmentation.

- Digital technology that continues to grow and intensify, which today can put human-type intelligence into inanimate objects such as cars, refrigerators and software that can write news stories.

- Uncommon competition — from outside once-protective national borders, and from outside once-unassailable industry boundaries.

I won't get deep into the intricacies of each one, because entire books have been written on them. A whole genre is devoted to VUCA (an acronym for volatility, uncertainty, complexity and ambiguity), coined in the late 1980s at the U.S. Army War College.[39] Rather, I will point to a few telling statistics to verify the forces. Then I'll show how they've conspired to make life very difficult for executives — but lucrative for the advisers they've hired to deal with them: consultants, lawyers, accountants, enterprise software companies, technology developers and troubleshooters, architects, and many others.

Customer Complexity

Businesses that sell to other organizations have customers who are much more knowledgeable and better prepared than they were 30 years ago — even five years ago — to evaluate them. Given the explosion of information on the web, your customers can easily go online and find a considerable amount about your business. What do your current and former employees think about your firm as a place to work? Just check out sites like Glassdoor.com or Vault.com. You'll see both good and bad reviews of your management, policies and practices. (For example, as I wrote this, McKinsey had more than 6,000 Glassdoor reviews, and software company Salesforce.com had more than 9,000.)[40]

If you haven't seen those sites before, be warned: Some comments may make you cringe. And, of course, your business customers can also learn about you from other customers who make comments to their friends, family members and business colleagues on popular social media sites like LinkedIn, Twitter and Facebook.

How does the increasing sophistication of your customers' customers make life more complex? It means your customers no longer can trade on the ignorance of *their* customers. Businesses like retailers, automotive manufacturers, airlines or software companies need expertise about how to sell to their smarter and more knowledgeable consumers. They will turn to advisers who can offer this expertise.

Moreover, the abundance of information that your clients' customers can glean for themselves online makes them more overwhelmed than ever, and increases the pressure on people who sell advice to be "sense-makers" of all that data, as Gartner's research has found.[41] Its extensive studies of corporate buying behavior found that after a certain amount of information, people go into brain overload and cling to what feels familiar and comforting: long-held beliefs, the status quo, cherry-picked data that confirms their points of view. In a world in which infinite data awaits online to be researched and over-researched, it's harder than ever to get people to buy your advice unless you can offer an irresistible solution that makes sense of it all. "The future belongs to those who can make sense of the ball of confusion," Gartner VP Maria Boulden said at a 2019 conference that I co-hosted.

This reality is faced by every business that sells products or services to other businesses in the last couple of decades. Your business customers' professional lives are roiled by greater complexity.

Consider a consulting firm named Urban Science. Most likely you haven't heard of it. But General Motors, Ford, Chrysler, Toyota, Volkswagen, Honda and every other automotive manufacturer that sells through dealerships have. Since 1977, Detroit-based Urban Science has been supplying its customers — automakers — with crucial information: where to locate their independently owned dealerships. (Urban Science's customers are car manufacturers, whose customers are car dealers, whose customers are you and me and other car buyers.) In 1977, company founder Jim Anderson, who's still the CEO, used that era's computer mapping technology to show Cadillac the best places in Chicago to locate dealerships among 37,000 potential Cadillac buyers.[42]

But since the World Wide Web took off in the 1990s, life has gotten much more difficult for Urban Science's customers — the automakers — and for the automakers' customers (the dealers) for the simple reason that the ultimate customers have grown far more knowledgeable about cars. They can go to online services such as TrueCar and Kelley Blue Book to get data on what they should pay for a car. They can even get data on the history of a specific used car.

One gauge on how complex life has gotten for automakers to understand their customers — in this case, dealers — is the growth of Urban Science. According to Dun & Bradstreet, the privately held firm is about a $60 million revenue business.[43] And Urban Science has more than 850 employees in 19 offices around the world.[44]

Digital Complexity

I cited the growth of the digital industry earlier. It's been one of the fastest-growing sectors on earth over the last 30 years. The internet economy has been growing too. In the U.S. in 2018, it made up 10 percent of GDP ($2.1 trillion) — nearly the same as the manufacturing sector did the year before. Also realize that by "internet economy," market watchers do *not* include companies that make the computer hardware, software and communications technologies that allow the sector to exist. They're only talking about companies like Amazon, Facebook, Google, wireless communications carriers (e.g., AT&T, Verizon) and the thousands of firms that do data processing, systems development and hosting of internet systems.[45]

What's more, consider that the internet industry effectively didn't exist before the first web browser hit the market in the early 1990s. Now it's the fourth largest sector in the U.S.[46]

What complexities does this spending on digital technology create for companies? At the very least, it forces executives to spend more time kicking the tires of technology vendors and service providers to implement the technology. While technology can help companies streamline processes and makes them more efficient, its greatest payback happens when managers rethink the way their departments do their work. This adds more complexity. And then, of course, people have to learn how to use new systems, and how to do their newly designed work differently and more productively. All to say, improving a company's operations is far more complex than it was 30 years ago.

Consider the marketing department. The soaring digital complexities in running a big marketing function may be a factor contributing to the falling tenure of CMOs in major advertisers. Marketing is no longer a game of bringing in an ad agency, asking "creatives" to come up with options, picking the best one, then letting media buyers decide in which print newspapers and magazines, TV shows and billboards to plaster the ads. Marketing campaigns are personalized today to what advertisers and their agencies can detect about their digital audiences.

In short, marketing today requires both Don Draper creativity and Albert Einstein science. To keep pace in a digital marketing world, the budgets for marketing technology alone shot up from 22 percent of the average marketing budget in 2017 to 29 percent in 2019, according to Gartner.[47] That's a far cry from the days when the marketing function's technology consisted of desktop computers and fax machines.

Digital complexities run rampant in every large (and small) company. Sorting through them to run a business more efficiently and effectively has become far more complex — if for no other reason than there are many more technologies to master, and many more business activities that need them. In turn, the demand for advice and other assistance in sorting through the digital complexities is huge.

Competitive Complexity

Executives in many industries have had to worry about being blindsided by companies that come out of left field. They are spooked by the story of Blockbuster Entertainment, which ignored Netflix until it was too late, and the magazine, newspaper and broadcast TV sectors that were left desolate by Facebook and Google. Online listings like Craigslist and online auction houses like eBay have stolen revenue from newspaper classified advertising sections. The global taxi industry didn't recognize Uber and Lyft for the threats they were until the tire tracks, so to say, were on the pavement.

The result: Determining exactly *who* a company competes against is a complex issue today. Rising competitive complexity — and failure to read the tea leaves — is why so many once-great and big companies are no longer with us, or are walking dead: Eastman Kodak, Toys R Us, Sears, Borders Books, Thomas Cook Travel, and many more that have filled the headlines of stories in the last 30 years.

In 2019, we helped one of our clients, Tata Consultancy Services (a $22 billion IT services and consulting firm), survey more than 1,000 executives at large companies in North America and Europe about how they look at competition and opportunities with customers. Every company had at least $1 billion in revenue. One in five of the companies no longer looked at their opportunities and threats solely within the age-old boundaries of their industry. They looked at opportunities (and competitors) from across industries, market-places that increasingly are referred to as "digital ecosystems."

Thinking of competition in terms of ecosystems rather than "competitors in our newspaper industry," or "competitors in the movie-making business" has enabled a number of new companies to destroy the biggies. When Netflix started in the late 1990s as a way to get movies to people who wanted to rent them, it skipped the video rental store and did it by taking orders online and mailing DVDs. But its co-founder Reed Hastings knew that distribution was only a way station until broadband internet service was everywhere — and once that happened, customers could download movies from Netflix online. Hastings realized long before the moment when broadband was prevalent that Netflix would be competing with other online distributors — particularly, the cable and telecommunications com-panies, many of which owned movie studios and produced program-ming. In the early 2000s, Netflix started producing its own movies. It has since become a big player in Hollywood.

That happened because Netflix didn't define its industry as "movie rental" 20 years ago. It's in the movie and TV production and distribution business. That's a digital ecosystem that now includes movie distribution as well as movie production. In the future, it could include digital advertising and online gaming, as some Netflix watchers observe.[48]

INTO THE COMPLEXITY VORTEX COME THE COMPLEXITY REDUCERS

With such complexities rising, is there any doubt why firms that greatly reduce them are able to get executive attention?

This is a key point, so let's walk through an example of a highly complex and high-stakes problem of a growing number of large companies: determining their digital strategy. In a world in which products and services can be reduced to bits and bytes, and then marketed, sold and distributed online, how should companies digitize their offerings? And then how can they create demand and supply for them through digital channels? This is a big concern for companies whose entire products can be turned into digital bits: retail banks (i.e., the product is money), media companies (all of which can be digitized) and insurers (don't need the paper of insurance forms), among many.

The complexity reducers for the digital strategy problem could include management consulting firms that help decode their clients' digital ecosystem strategy. But the complexity reducers also can be law firms that help companies decide where they need patents to slow down competitors.

The complexity reducers can also be architecture firms that demonstrate why a client's management team must redesign offices for highly creative and rigorous planning ideas to flourish. Or the complexity reducers can be software companies that provide systems that rapidly summon information customers need on their smartphones to purchase their services.

Or the complexity reducers can be investment banking firms that help companies understand which firms in adjoining sectors they should buy in order to rule their digital ecosystem. And then, of course, they can be the ones that do the deal transactions.

Sounds right, you might be saying. But you may also be asking why traditional marketing is not likely to help the consulting, law or architecture firm or investment bank get in the door to solve these complex problems. As complexity reducers, they must demonstrate

— before they're brought in at a hefty price — that they have the expertise that solves their target clients' problems. Simply proclaiming they have the requisite expertise in an advertisement or on the golf course isn't enough anymore. It's not convincing. With so much at stake in solving their biggest problem, companies need to trust that a solution provider has superior expertise in solving it.

Proclaiming such expertise through advertisements, trade show booths, sales brochures and slick website pages that describe a company's services and products works only when those products — and the problems they solve — are not complex. It works when you're selling automobiles or bananas or cameras or phones. They're not complex products for customers to comprehend.

In contrast, consulting advice, legal counsel, enterprise software, and financial and other complex solutions to complex problems are very difficult for customers to understand. And they can require big investments. That makes them high-cost, high-stakes purchases.

I like to show executives the "spaces" within which companies need thought leadership — and the spaces in which traditional brand and product/service marketing are more appropriate. A way to think about these spaces is to map it on a grid of complexity — the vertical axis being the complexity of the problem that some product/service addresses (i.e., your customer's problem), and the horizontal axis being the complexity of the solution (i.e., your product and/or service offering).[49] With these axes, you can plot every company's marketing approach into three zones of complexity:

- **Image marketing** (low problem complexity/low solution complexity): Products and services that are simple for customers to understand and that solve simple problems are sold on the basis of a brand image that a company creates.

Starbucks' brand image is one of sophistication of a simple product and experience: tasteful and educated. Since the problems (e.g., thirst) and solutions (e.g., a beverage) are easy for customers to understand, marketing must be more about creating an emotional experience with the product — not about going into detail on the product specifications. Companies such as Coca-Cola (with slogans over the years such as "It's the Real Thing," "I'd Like to Buy the World a Coke" and "Always Coca-Cola") and Pepsi ("Right Now" and "Generation Next" in the 1990s, and its more recent tagline, "That's What I Like") are masters of image marketing.

- **Product marketing** (medium problem complexity/medium solution complexity): Products that are well known but which compete on the basis of features and functions are in this category. Think about cars, homes and refrigerators. If you want a car that runs on little fuel and has safety features you believe are critical, you will likely do vehicle-by-vehicle comparisons: mileage, battery life (if electric or hybrid), backup cameras, lane departure warning, etc.

- **Thought leadership marketing** (high problem complexity/high solution complexity): In these cases, the target customer can have a hard time even defining the problem, and they're often bewildered about how to solve it.

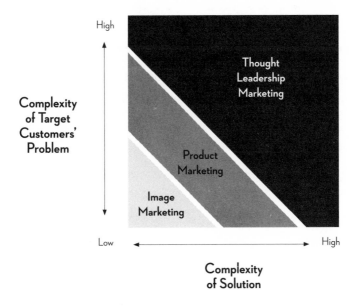

If you are selling your products and services in the high-problem complexity/high-solution complexity zone, then you are competing on thought leadership. Your target audience will want you to show them your expertise — through articles, books and blog posts they can read; and through conference presentations on site or via video.

I've seen many B2B companies get confused about when they need image, product and thought leadership marketing. One large company once ran an extensive thought leadership campaign for a new service offering using the image marketing channel of print advertising. It had full-page ads that looked like a long op-ed. In other words, the company used a high-bias, low-bandwidth marketing channel to try to convey a low-bias, high-bandwidth message (a concept I expand on in Chapter 7). For thought leadership content, this is not optimal.

So now you've read about the forces that have made life a lot more complicated for your business customers. Their executives are hungry for insights that make complicated matters comprehensible. That has opened the door wide for thought leaders.

But exactly how thought leaders become thought leaders is what we'll explain in the next and subsequent chapters.

PART II

ORGANIZING AND STEERING THOUGHT LEADERSHIP

CHAPTER 3

DEVISING A THOUGHTFUL THOUGHT LEADERSHIP STRATEGY

+   +   +   +   +   +   +   +

MAGINE YOU OVERSEE THE $2 billion-a-year U.S. marketing budget of Ford Motor Company.[50] Marketing decisions are made at both the corporate level where you work, and at the divisional levels (Mercury, Ford, etc.). At the start of each year, you tell the divisional marketing heads how much of the total marketing pie they'll get for advertising, public relations, sports sponsorships and other programs. But a month later, odd things start happening. You see expensive ad campaigns pop up on national TV, media websites and print magazines for products that are trivial for Ford from a revenue standpoint. You worry that those divisional marketing chiefs may shell out more on marketing than Ford will actually generate from selling the vehicles to Ford dealers.

Yet you haven't seen the worst of the marketing mistakes. Two months later, you see a loud, flashy TV commercial for a car that you know is no fewer than five years away, maybe 10. Or maybe never. It's one of those concept models that auto manufacturers unveil at big car shows or in car magazines to gauge the "wow" impact — i.e., are consumers impressed? But again, it's a concept car that may never arrive at any Ford dealer anywhere.

Of course, that scenario is not at all likely to happen at Ford — or at any other auto company. It's not likely to occur at any large consumer products company for that matter — especially for products in the concept stage. Throwing tons of marketing money at marginal products, or products that are just concepts, is simply absurd.

Nonetheless, I'm not exaggerating when I say that this goes on in many B2B firms that throw thought leadership marketing dollars around like they're fertilizer on a golf course. And when I say dollars, I mean actual money going out the door to print and distribute articles, publish books, run conferences and hire PR firms. I also mean the dollar value of the time that a firm's fee-generating professionals spend to become recognized as thought leaders — time they could devote to generating and delivering billable work.

CAUTION AHEAD: THE COST OF A POOR THOUGHT LEADERSHIP STRATEGY

Scenarios like these happen when a firm has no thought leadership strategy, or one that is half-baked and disconnected from the services the company sells to clients. Many B2B firms have no rhyme or reason as to why certain low-revenue parts of their business are making outsized investments in thought leadership, while other, higher-revenue parts are spending very little. Over the years, I've seen companies spend up to a million dollars or more on research, a book, article placements, seminars and conference speeches to develop and promote a concept that no one else in the firm practices — other than that team.

Think about that for a second. Consider a hypothetical consulting firm that has revenue of $100 million, employs 300 consultants, and spends $5 million a year on thought leadership marketing. (For a company of that size, $5 million would be an average budget, based on our research.) Early in the year, two partners convince the managing partner they have a great concept for a new service. "Every client who has heard about it loves it," they tell him. The two partners are given a budget of $1 million over the next 12 months to conduct two studies, publish a book, retain a top-tier PR firm, launch a journal, and run seminars and webinars. All of a sudden, 20 percent of the chief marketing officer's $5 million budget is gone . . . to create demand for a service that has yet to pull in any business.

This is a sign of a thought leadership strategy that is out of control, the victim of a costly pet project. I've seen numerous variations of this story. They're so common that I'm no longer shocked by them.

Our research suggests this may be the rule, not the exception. Over the past several years, we've collaborated with Jason Mlicki — the marketing whiz who runs Rattleback and who has been my intellectual partner in five thought leadership conferences — on several studies of thought leadership practices. Our 2020 survey of 314 thought leadership marketers in North American, European and Asian-Pacific B2B companies found only 24 percent had allocated their investments in proportion to their services' revenue contribution.[51]

Why does this happen with thought leadership investments? Three reasons. The first is that thought leadership activities can easily go underground while product marketing activities are more visible. A partner gives a speech at a conference. Nobody else at the company hears it. It may not even show up as an expense if the conference organizer paid for the partner's speech and the travel expenses. In contrast, a car company runs a commercial for a vehicle in prime time. Everyone at the firm — including millions of TV viewers — can see it, either on the show or on YouTube later. The ad agency's bill will soon be visible to the car company's finance officer.

In other words, many thought leadership activities don't have to be staged by a central marketing group or with their help. The rise of social media sites such as LinkedIn, Twitter and Medium.com enables a company's experts to take marketing into their own hands. They can — and do — post messages and articles on those sites. When marketing tries to stop such activities, consulting firm consultants, law firm attorneys, architecture firm architects and other professionals will push back, arguing that they're not spending marketing's budget. Or they contend that they're not advertising; they're educating the target audience. Or they're not crafting advertising copy that needs to be polished or win awards; they're just informing their audience.

It's difficult for company marketers to control experts who go rogue like this — especially if they are encouraging them to become recognized as thought leaders.

The second reason why thought leadership spending can go askew is related to the first, but is different: These investments can be buried deep in service and product line budgets. I remember hearing from a client a few years ago — a senior executive at a Big Four accounting and consulting firm — that his firm could track $50 million that it spends annually on thought leadership programs in the U.S. But he didn't have a clue about the companies' global numbers.

If they're not embedded in service, product or regional budgets, thought leadership expenses are often folded into sales and business development budgets. In either case, they're essentially underground activities.

The third way I've seen thought leadership investments get out of whack is when influential experts in the firm pull rank. They often are partners with big Rolodexes and large books of business. Once they become recognized in the marketplace as thought leaders, their personal stock goes way up. If they have little loyalty to the firm that funded their eminence-building programs, they can walk out the door and bring their new-found personal brand affinity to a competitor.

But those aren't the only problems that could befall a firm without a solid thought leadership strategy. There are several others.

IMPACTS OF POOR THOUGHT LEADERSHIP STRATEGIES

One is what I call "content cacophony." The Merriam-Webster dictionary defines cacophony as the "harshness in the sound of words or phrases; an incongruous or chaotic mixture." Content cacophony happens when one part of a firm says the solution to a customer problem is X, and another part of the firm says it's Y — and that X is not the right solution.

This, no doubt, is troublesome. A company whose cacophonous messages make a complex issue even more confusing is a company without an effective thought leadership strategy.

Another consequence of a weak thought leadership strategy can be poor content that your audience rejects or ignores. Have the following things happened to you?

- Your white papers aren't extensively downloaded. But even if they are, they don't generate many inquiries from prospects.

- You promote webinars and seminars and very few people show up to hear them — people who could actually buy your services.

- Editors at key publications keep rejecting your opinion article submissions.

- Your speaker submissions to important conferences get turned down — other than at conferences that demand a speaking fee.

These are all signs that a firm's content isn't good enough. They're signals that the people a company uses to help its experts get their expertise "on paper" aren't skilled enough, or aren't given the necessary authority, or don't have effective approaches, tools and processes for turning the experts' knowledge into clear or compelling arguments. Or these people could be effective, yet the firm's subject experts don't give them adequate time and compelling insights.

Our research and other research show that mediocre content is the rule, not the exception. In our 2020 survey of thought leadership marketers, only 26 percent said their firms produce high-quality content. Even the biggest firms surveyed ($5 billion or more in revenue) struggle to bring compelling content to market. Only 35 percent of them said their content was of high quality.

Remember what I said in Chapter 2: Thought leadership content must make the complex coherent. And the place where coherence begins is with a thoughtful thought leadership strategy.

But how does a firm devise one? Let's dive into that.

THE FOUR ELEMENTS OF THOUGHT LEADERSHIP STRATEGY

Like any sound strategy, a thought leadership strategy must help a firm channel its resources (people, budget, programs) to the right places. It must lay out four elements:

1. **The core problems of target clients that the firm will "own."** This not only includes the types of organizations that need its expertise but also exactly who in those organizations need it, and to solve exactly what problems.

2. **How the firm will develop exceptional content about solving those core client problems.** This must include where the firm will need research to produce new expertise and services that it doesn't currently have, and where it will need to codify the expertise it already has.

3. **How to create demand for the firm's expertise.** This is about building a sizable audience of prospects, and converting enough of them into clients, in order for a firm to achieve its growth goals.

4. **How to ramp up services that solve those problems.** That is, how to convert the content into new services, or into new approaches for existing services, and ensure quality.

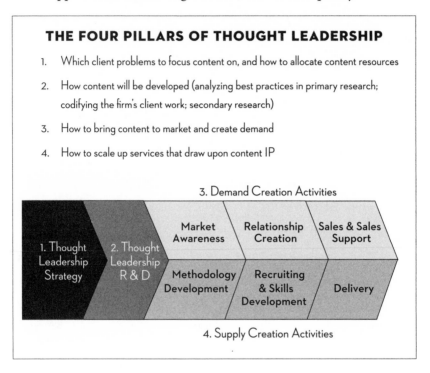

THE FOUR PILLARS OF THOUGHT LEADERSHIP

1. Which client problems to focus content on, and how to allocate content resources

2. How content will be developed (analyzing best practices in primary research; codifying the firm's client work; secondary research)

3. How to bring content to market and create demand

4. How to scale up services that draw upon content IP

3. Demand Creation Activities

| 1. Thought Leadership Strategy | 2. Thought Leadership R & D | Market Awareness | Relationship Creation | Sales & Sales Support |
| | | Methodology Development | Recruiting & Skills Development | Delivery |

4. Supply Creation Activities

The chapters that follow will go into more detail about how to execute these four elements of thought leadership. But they all should begin with an effective thought leadership strategy. Let's look at its core.

Target Clients' Problems to Own

Determining which client problems to focus on is at the heart of thought leadership strategy. Jeanne Thompson, a speaker from our 2018 "Profiting from Thought Leadership" conference (and, at the time, SVP of thought leadership at Fidelity Investments), called these the client problems to "own," adding that thought leadership marketers must "fall in love with those problems."[52]

Those are great words — "fall in love with those problems." The reason is that it's easy for thought leaders to wander over time away from the client problems they first decided to "own." Many CSC Index consultants told me they were bored after being staffed on their sixth or seventh reengineering project. Company leaders started delving into other areas — business strategy, product innovation and other client problems for which CSC Index had little depth in solving.

In the early 2000s, a few years after I left CSC Index, the firm I co-owned (Bloom Group) was brought in to help a finance consulting company establish its thought leadership strategy. It had become a $10 million revenue firm by focusing on one core client problem: helping chief financial officers make their departments more operationally effective. After its purchase by a much larger professional services company, the financial consulting firm felt pressure to sharply increase its growth. The result was disastrous: It strayed beyond solving its core client problems (finance department operational improvement) to try to help other business functions (sales, marketing, R&D) better manage their budgets. We told the firm's new CEO to categorize the firm's projects over the previous 10 years, then track how much revenue each project brought in and whether the client would be likely to provide a reference on the quality of the consulting firm's work.

What we found was striking: 90 percent of the firm's revenue came from solving the original client problem (finance department operations improvement), and 10 percent came from helping other business functions become more fiscally prudent. What's more, most of the finance improvement projects were referenceable, while most of the business function work was not. We told the firm's management that their first thought leadership strategy decision was about determining which client problem they wanted to own, and that as a $10 million firm they couldn't own the large number of problems they had been pursuing.

The client problems that a firm decides to own should be persistent problems, unless some breakthrough technology miraculously makes them disappear. And even though a company's superior solution may work for a while — and may even become celebrated through its thought leadership marketing — it will not likely solve the problem forever. Like a virus, a problem will continue to mutate and outwit even the smartest solutions. Companies that sell advice must keep innovating. They need to stay in love with the problems of their target clients that they've chosen to own — but invent new and improved ways to solve them.

As the first step in setting an effective thought leadership strategy, a firm must decide where it wants to be seen as the expert. This means not only identifying specific problems where its expertise provides the best solutions, but also specifying how many of these problems they can "own." Ideally, the firm will have an overall business strategy that has decided this: "We solve these client problems, but not those."

Without focusing on the right problems to own, a firm's thought leadership spending can be grossly misallocated. It's like having an untended backyard garden. Over a summer, certain plants and flowers take over and crowd out others. Keeping the garden in shape requires cutting some plants back, and watering and fertilizing the ones you want to flourish with more intention.

Nonetheless, many B2B firms do not have an explicit thought leadership strategy. Perhaps it's because they fear they can't be opportunistic — that is, they'll have to turn away revenue from outside their core when it shows up. Or maybe they believe that all they need to do is hire someone with the expertise to solve a client problem that their firm hasn't solved before — even if it's far from the expertise it has delivered in the past.

Given that it can be difficult to buck such sentiments at the top, we advise chief marketing officers and heads of thought leadership not to clash with top management over this issue. But what we do tell them is to get top management to agree on where to funnel corporate thought leadership resources — on the main client problems the firm has decided to own. That requires a top-down and bottom-up thought leadership strategy.

OPTIMAL TL STRATEGY:
Top-Down *and* Bottom-Up Driven

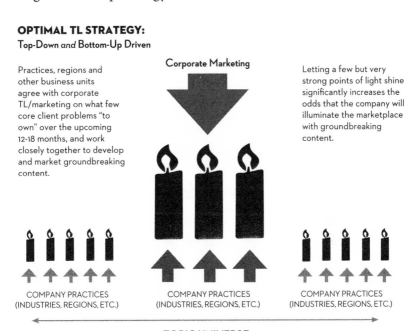

Practices, regions and other business units agree with corporate TL/marketing on what few core client problems "to own" over the upcoming 12-18 months, and work closely together to develop and market groundbreaking content.

Corporate Marketing

Letting a few but very strong points of light shine significantly increases the odds that the company will illuminate the marketplace with groundbreaking content.

COMPANY PRACTICES
(INDUSTRIES, REGIONS, ETC.)

COMPANY PRACTICES
(INDUSTRIES, REGIONS, ETC.)

COMPANY PRACTICES
(INDUSTRIES, REGIONS, ETC.)

TOPIC UNIVERSE

In this case, a CMO or head of thought leadership works with company leaders to identify the core client problems that thought leadership people will focus their budget on. That's the top-down piece. In the meantime, thought leadership activities by practices outside the core are allowed to continue. But they won't get substantial, if any, corporate resources. Sure, if they have their own budgets, they can spend it on articles, LinkedIn posts, speeches and other thought leadership marketing. In the meantime, corporate marketing is watering the plants that company leaders believe will need continual tending.

What is less optimal is having an all-controlling top-down thought leadership strategy that prevents experts outside the core from creating demand for their services. Those experts will quickly see corporate marketing as the enemy if they are prevented from publishing. You don't want to stifle grassroots attempts at thought leadership. It will disenfranchise them, and it could stifle ideas that might grow into attractive services.

Conversely, you don't want anarchy to be your thought leadership strategy either. That's where a corporate marketing or thought leadership function becomes an order-taker, publishing anything and everything that practice leaders tell them to publish, with no or few core client problems in mind.

WHEN YOU HAVE A WEAK OR NO CORPORATE TL STRATEGY

Practices, regions and other business units largely publish and market what they want, with little cooperation or help from the Corporate Marketing/TL.

Corporate Marketing

Core Topics

Letting a thousand points of light shine results in no strong light.

Bottom-Up TL Strategy

COMPANY PRACTICES (INDUSTRIES, REGIONS, ETC.)

TOPIC UNIVERSE

A firm can focus its thought leadership investments only if it has an explicit idea of which client problems it must own. Our 2020 research found that the most effective thought leadership marketers were nearly four times more likely to have done this than the least effective marketers. Some 60 percent of the most effective ones allocated their investments by the revenue contribution and growth potential of their practices. Only 16 percent of the least effective thought leadership marketers did that.

ESTABLISHING OVERALL CONTENT DEVELOPMENT PROCESSES

After deciding where to focus, CMOs and heads of thought leadership then need to determine standards for content quality and how the company will meet them. By quality standards, we mean the quality of the ideas in articles, white papers, conference presentations, books and the like. In the next chapter we'll go deeply into criteria that we have found to matter most. But in a thought leadership strategy, company leaders must agree on two things:

- **They need an objective set of standards for content quality, in order to recognize whether content is ready to go to market.** Our research has found that most thought leadership marketers have explicit and shared content quality standards, and that they enforce them.

- **The processes and resources required to develop high-quality content.** Which client problems require the firm to conduct primary research to come up with compelling solutions? Which client problems require the firm to merely collect and codify the expertise it's delivered for years? We'll cover this in the next chapter as well.

DETERMINING OVERALL DEMAND CREATION

This is the demand side of thought leadership. The content that a firm creates and markets represents a promise to the marketplace — that it has sufficient expertise to solve clients' problems.

Creating demand will take a range of marketing and sales activities. Those activities will work best if they are designed to work together and gently lead prospective clients to your firm. Jill Kramer, chief marketing and communications officer of Accenture, said it best at a 2020 conference my firm co-hosted, when she noted that Accenture's thought leadership research "is not a journey to a PDF; it's a journey to a conversation."[53]

Those "demand-creation" activities will necessarily have to be designed so that the target client has a highly effective educational experience — all the way from the initial read of an article to a review of the content on the firm's website, to listening to the experts at a webinar or seminar, to a discussion with a business development person.

DETERMINING OVERALL SUPPLY CREATION

While content development, marketing and salespeople are creating and handling demand, others in a firm need to be handling supply — i.e., ramping up the firm's ability to deliver on the promises of its thought leadership messages.

B2B firms will need to build those capabilities, by developing methodologies, recruiting people who can do the work and training them on how to master the methodologies they've created.

From nearly 40 years of experience, I have seen thought leadership executives spend far more time and money on the content development and demand generation end of thought leadership, and much less on the supply side: developing service offerings or new approaches to existing services.

Remember, thought leadership marketing makes promises to prospective clients — that your firm has superior services for solving certain problems of theirs. Your firm must be ready to deliver those capabilities to the marketplace if it is to grow and compete on the basis of thought leadership. Otherwise, you're no better than the automaker that dazzles you with concept cars that never come to market.

The four elements of a sound thought leadership strategy should guide your thought leadership investments and keep your activities apportioned appropriately. Your strategy must also put the right content development activities in place. It must design the optimal marketing mix to create demand. And it should lay out the methodology development, recruiting and internal training activities that will help you scale up your services.

I've provided depth in this chapter on the first element — determining what problems of your target clients to "own." I'll go deeper on ways to execute content development, demand creation, and supply creation in subsequent chapters.

Once you create a sound strategy, you are on a solid path to taking what I call a *content-centric* rather than a *marketing-centric* approach to thought leadership. That's an elemental step to compete on the basis of thought leadership.

PART III

CREATING BREAKTHROUGH IDEAS

CHAPTER 4

WHY CONTENT MUST BE KING

+   +   +   +   +   +   +   +

THIS CHAPTER AND THE next two are about what's at the center of a company's ability to compete on thought leadership: great content. In turn, great content is the product of developing and codifying a superior solution to a client problem. To get there you need a combination of primary best-practice research, uncommon insights about your research findings and proven results from putting those findings to use with clients.

To compete on thought leadership, companies must have a *content-centric* mindset and a *content-centric* approach to developing expertise. Many firms think marketing their content should be the first priority. That will be fruitless, and I'll explain why in this chapter.

Great content rules. But what constitutes great content? We see nine qualities. They should guide top executives who must decide which of the company's approaches and services are ready for the critical gaze of the marketplace and have the potential to attract the most clients. These attributes also should shape the thought leadership marketers' work — to hone the thinking of their firms' experts and craft the components of their thought leadership strategy. How well your ideas stack up against these benchmarks will show whether you need deeper thinking, more research or more field experiences to make it ready.

Let's look at these nine qualities.

THE NINE HALLMARKS OF COMPELLING CONTENT

Whether it's based on research or a firm's field experience with clients, what makes the content appealing? How do we know when it is good — at least, good enough that we don't need any more from our experts to make it better? What criteria must it meet?

The criteria that I lay out are important for everyone involved in thought leadership in your firm to remember, agree on and internalize. This applies to your company's current and up-and-coming thought leaders, your editorial people, your marketing people and your salespeople. If those factions don't agree on the criteria, they are likely to argue about whether an idea is good enough to take to market. Or if a campaign falls short of expectations, they'll blame the marketers for not doing enough marketing, rather than the content people for not making the content good enough.

These disagreements will be debilitating. They will set back your firm's thought leadership programs and your personal relationships with the people in it. To avoid such setbacks, you will need to agree on exactly what constitutes compelling thought leadership content. The most resonant ideas I've seen share nine traits. They are:

- Relevant

- Novel

- Deep

- Feasible to implement

- Evidence-based

- Illuminating

- Irrefutable

- Clear

- Stimulating

THE 9 ELEMENTS OF EXCEPTIONAL CONTENT

Component	Explanation
1. Highly **relevant** problem	Extremely timely problem for target audience
2. **Novel** solution	Solution is very different than others in the market
3. **Depth** of understanding problem/explicating	Developed or detailed analysis
4. **Feasible and visible** solution	Lays out key elements and steps of solving the problem
5. **Evidence** that solution works and is superior to others	Case study, statistics, and other validations that organizations which adopted the solution got better results
6. **Illuminating**	Uses frameworks to simplify complex issues, data visualization (e.g., digital charts), and other devices for making sense of complex matters.
7. **Irrefutable**	Unassailable logic in every aspect of problem and solution
8. **Clarity** of argument	Overall argument is easily understood by target audience
9. **Stimulating**	Provides intriguing and little-known facts that support argument

You can read how I define them in the greater context of thought leadership on the previous page. But it might be helpful to explain why they are fundamental to being seen as a leading expert.

If a company publishes content on a problem no one knows about, if it can't prove the problem is serious or soon will be, why would anyone care? Let's say you can give me an incisive white paper that claims it's a big problem that only a minority of people wear digital watches. If your paper hasn't proven *why* this is a problem for me, I won't read it. It's not relevant to me.

Having a novel solution is as important as having a real, here-and-now problem. If a firm is essentially prescribing the same thing that three other firms have prescribed, why would a fourth solution matter to anyone?

When a solution is novel, it will attract attention. And if you can show that it actually has had beneficial impact, it will heighten that attention. That is where having evidence comes in.

EVIDENCE: WHY YOU NEED IT, AND HOW TO GET IT

The most important element in becoming recognized as a thought leader is evidence — proof that your solution to a certain client problem actually works, and works well. If you don't have such evidence, you won't have convincing content. Evidence is at the heart of thought leadership content, and content is at the heart of generating recognition and revenue from expertise.

The best way to get this evidence is also the hardest: getting multiple companies to share their success stories, demonstrating that your solution is superior to others. I'm not likely to get into your rocket ship if you haven't test-piloted it first. Executives don't like to be guinea pigs for novel solutions. They want those that have been proven to work.

With reengineering, Michael Hammer and CSC Index could trot out a more than dozen real-life case examples of companies that had redesigned a key business process and achieved quantum improvements in revenue, costs, time to market and quality. Those companies included Hallmark Cards, IBM Credit, Mutual Benefit Life Insurance and Progressive Insurance. Those case studies were worth their weight in gold. They were extremely valuable evidence that reengineering actually worked. These case examples attracted Fortune 500 CEOs to CSC Index and Hammer like moths to an outdoor light bulb.

This kind of case research has been behind the success of Jim Collins' preeminence as a management thinker for the last 30 years. His first mega-bestselling business book (*Built to Last*, co-authored with Jerry Porras) was based on their six years of research at Stanford University's business school. They compared companies that were highly successful in the 1980s and 1990s (including 3M, Procter & Gamble, Merck, Disney and Walmart) against a comparative set of lackluster companies in their sectors. Collins based his next bestseller (*Good to Great*) on five years of research. His approach to thought leadership echoes the approach that Hammer and CSC Index took: comparing the best and the worst companies on a topic. Collins describes this process so well on his website: "Turning mountains of data into useful concepts is an iterative process of looping back and forth, developing ideas and testing them against the data, revising the ideas, building a framework, seeing it break under the weight of evidence, and rebuilding it yet again."[54]

In fact, the most important criterion for thought leadership is evidence that the prescribed solution actually works. That's why it's worth explaining this in more detail — in essence, giving you the evidence to understand why evidence is important! Lawyers need evidence to win cases. To get regulatory approval, pharmaceutical companies need proof that patients are significantly improved by a new drug in clinical trials, and with few harmful side effects. Automakers spend lots of time hoping their *Consumer Reports* and J.D. Power vehicle quality ratings are good. They know that many educated consumers are looking for proof of quality in selecting vehicles.

It's easy to craft a novel argument about a new way to solve a problem. But if it doesn't hold the water of evidence, it's not a powerful argument — it's just an intriguing theory. Smart executives, with their careers and the fortunes of their company on the line, don't buy theory.

So where can you get that evidence? It can come from two sources: your firm's successful client work or primary research on companies that (when you delve into their stories) used a solution like the one you are proposing. Sometimes you may need a combination of both.

You should use these two sources to create case examples, which are somewhere in between case studies (but without going into a deep examination of the type that a Harvard Business School case study would go into) and anecdotes of the type you will read in business publication feature stories.

Case examples are not easy to collect. Why? First, you need to find them. That can take days of extensive web searching. And even if you have client work that fits the bill of "best practice," that client work typically is confidential. Without permission from your clients, you can't disclose how you've helped them. This is where most B2B companies I've known give up. They say something like, "Our client work is confidential. They won't allow us to go public with it, so it's not worth asking them." I'm sure it is, and for nearly four decades I've helped my clients secure the permission of many of their clients to go public with their stories.

How? By positioning their case example as a *best-practice story* that shows the wisdom of their executives — not as a *client testimonial* of the value of their services. That's a huge difference. If you say, "Look, we're looking to support our research or a white paper with best-practice examples of companies that have addressed a certain business problem. We'd like to feature your company, and we will give you editorial control over what is said about you," you'd be surprised how many clients will say yes. It can be very good PR for their company — and for their own careers.

The value of such case stories to your target audience, and the difficulty in collecting them, makes them worth their weight in gold. When you've got them, you've built a moat against competitors who don't have their own or as many.

ILLUMINATION: CREATING ENDURING FRAMEWORKS THAT SIMPLIFY COMPLEXITY

An idea is truly illuminating if it has frameworks that simplify complex issues. Hammer and CSC Index's "reengineering diamond" helped to make the concept "click" with audiences. It described the interrelationships among business processes, jobs and work, values and beliefs, and information technology in a reengineered business process. Jim Collins has brought many classic frameworks to the business world: level 5 leadership, the flywheel and the hedgehog concept, among others.

Great frameworks create coherence out of confusion, according to Dave Ulrich, a guru on human capability issues (talent, organization, leadership and human resources) in large organizations for the last 30 years. He has created many leading frameworks over that time. "Simplifying ideas forces clarity and allows for the ideas to have impact," said Ulrich, a longtime professor at the University of Michigan's Ross School of Business and a partner at the consulting firm the RBL Group.[55]

One of my favorite frameworks was created by a client, FMG Leading, a human capital strategy firm that helps healthcare and private equity firms develop strong leaders at all levels. (It's one of several consulting practices at FMG Leading.) It published a foundational point of view and a 2017 *Harvard Business Review* article about how hospital systems and other healthcare services firms should develop the skills of physicians who take on leadership roles.

PHYSICIAN LEADER PIPELINE - SKILL REQUIREMENTS

LEADERSHIP RESPONSIBILITY				
Enterprise MD Leader	Relational	Business	Strategic	
Group MD Leader	Clinical	Relational	Business	Strategic
Market MD Leader	Clinical	Relational	Business	Strategic
MD Leader	Clinical		Relational	Business
Individual Practitioner	Clinical			Relational

Source: FMG Leading

The framework quickly clarifies a complex idea: the four fundamental skills that physicians need to rise into bigger and bigger jobs.[56] That makes the authors' advice easy to grasp.[57]

RIGOR AND CLARITY MAKE YOUR ARGUMENT AIRTIGHT AND UNDERSTOOD

When you lay out a problem and position your company's solution as the best one, your argument must be airtight. If it has holes, your readers are not going to fill them for you. You must make your argument bulletproof before you unveil it to the world, no matter how excited and impatient you may be to launch it into the marketplace.

Along with being rigorously supported, your argument must also be understood by your audience. This will likely mean using different language than the language you use with your colleagues: concepts and terms your audience understands. (This is why thought leadership seems to have become the full employment act for journalists and other writers.)

The presentation of little-known facts that support the dissection of a problem and better solution to it is another hallmark of thought-leading content. Such intriguing details can turn a dense, serious topic into a more enjoyable one. They can go a long way toward making a potentially dry topic highly interesting.

Here's an example: An HR consulting firm called Talent Dimensions conducted case research and wrote a report in 2017 on how companies can determine which people are the most important ones to retain. Through extensive secondary research, it found that Google paid $650 million in 2014 to buy a UK startup company with 50 computer scientists specializing in artificial intelligence.[58] That princely sum was revealing — that certain people in companies hold jobs that are far more valuable to organizational success than other jobs, and that these jobs were not necessarily in the C-suite.

With these nine criteria in hand, you can have more fruitful discussions in your company about whether an article is ready to be published, a research study has been sufficiently analyzed and communicated well enough, or a conference presentation is ready for its audience. You'll be taking typically subjective discussions — "This article isn't very good, and I just can't put my finger on why" — that raise tension and can warp relationships, and making them far less subjective. In fact, you'll be making them objective — if everyone agrees with the criteria.

More important, you'll have the means to help your aspiring thought leaders to improve their ideas rather than simply reject them with vague criticism. Feedback like, "We lack three convincing case examples," or "We don't have enough evidence that the problem is widespread," or "We need an incisive framework by which clients can diagnose the problem the same way we diagnose it," is precious to experts who are willing to accept it to develop their core argument.

DETERMINING HOW TO DEVELOP YOUR CONTENT

If you understand what makes content compelling, it then becomes easier to understand what you will need to develop compelling content. The first determination is understanding whether you need primary research, or whether capturing your company's field experience will be sufficient.

Content Criteria	Field Experience	Primary Research
Relevance of problem	Target audience is widely aware of problem	Target audience may need to be convinced they have a problem
Novelty of your existing solution	High (very novel)	Low (not novel); other solutions are more novel
Evidence that your solution works	Sufficient evidence	Insufficient evidence
Depth	Low number of competing and viable solutions	Significant number of competing and viable solutions
Feasibility	Deep understanding of superior solution and how to implement it	Shallow (if any) understanding of superior solution and how to implement it
Rigor	Baseline Criteria	Baseline Criteria
Illumination	Baseline Criteria	Baseline Criteria
Clarity	Baseline Criteria	Baseline Criteria
Stimulating	Baseline Criteria	Baseline Criteria

Use the table above to diagnose the state of your firm's expertise on a core client problem. Answer these questions honestly and thoroughly — seeing what competitors have already published before deciding whether your concept is high on the novelty dimension, has sufficient evidence that it works, and so on.

Once you do that evaluation, it will become clear which of your firm's solutions will be supported by its field experience, and which will require primary research.

Client problem by client problem, you could then map out a portfolio of content development initiatives. You'd decide where your firm's expertise stands on each one, and which ones need primary research and which ones simply require capturing the field experience of your firm's client work.

WHY IT'S A MISTAKE TO PUT MARKETING BEFORE CONTENT

Unfortunately, many firms that strive to be seen as thought leaders do not believe their ideas need rigor, primary research or field experience to get there. In their minds, it is a luxury — a nice-to-have when business is booming and budgets are flush. This mentality often prevails when marketing controls the content development function, or when there is no thought leadership research function at all.

It's part of what I call a *marketing-centric* view on thought leadership. This mindset treats thought leadership as a marketing game — as more or less quickly capturing the thoughts of an expert or two, getting it down in a document and launching it into the marketplace. Capturing the expertise is the trivial part, this thinking goes; the marketing of it is where the real work is.

Unfortunately, the marketing-centric view of thought leadership dominates today. And I have research — not just client experience — to support this assertion.

YET THE MARKETING-CENTRIC APPROACH PREVAILS

The 2020 study I mentioned in the previous chapter, of more than 300 thought leadership professionals (three quarters of them marketers), gives statistical validity to something I've seen in dozens of companies since the late 1980s. It's that the majority of thought leadership marketers believe the most important element for a firm to become known for its expertise is marketing programs that attract prospects to some piece of content — not the content itself. Today, those marketing programs include social media messaging (Twitter, LinkedIn, etc.), email newsletters that mention and link to the content, and media outreach that gets reporters to mention the content in their stories.

In our survey we asked which one factor (of four) was most important in their best thought leadership campaign of the previous three years:

- Was it having an engaging experience on the firm's website that enables viewers who are moved by some content to quickly set up a conversation with the authors?

- Was it having salespeople who were knowledgeable enough about the content to be able to get a good percentage of prospects to buy something?

- Was it well-orchestrated marketing programs that drove people to the firm's thought leadership content on its website, or to reach out directly to them?

- Or was it having exceptional content — i.e., truly compelling insights?

We didn't allow them to answer "all are important," "two are equally important" or "three are equally important." They had to choose one.

By far, the most popular answer was the third option: effective marketing programs. Some 51 percent chose that one, far ahead of the second-ranking option, exceptional content. Only 28 percent picked that. The other two responses each were chosen by 10 percent of our participants.

Marketing, in their minds, trumps content.

This is problematic. In thought leadership, content trumps marketing. Maybe this belies my bias in thought leadership. I've always been a content person. I'm attracted to substance, not sizzle. I love discovering richly supported and groundbreaking ideas that change the market conversation.

By the way, I am by no means alone. In the survey I just mentioned, we did find that content was put on a similarly high pedestal as marketing by the most effective practitioners of thought leadership. This group constituted 18 percent of our survey base. In answer to our question about how effective their thought leadership activities were at generating recognition and leads for business, they all said, "extremely effective." On the question that forced them to rank the most important element of thought leadership success, 38 percent said "content" and 40 percent said marketing.

I should also note that the least effective companies at thought leadership were more than twice as likely to be marketing-centric than content-centric. Of the companies that said their thought leadership marketing was ineffective, 59 percent said that marketing was the most important factor in their thought leadership campaign. Only 27 percent said content was the reason.

This is not to minimize the need for excellent marketing. That is essential to having an audience learn about a bold new idea. But that marketing is likely to be ineffective if the content isn't stellar. To compete on thought leadership, B2B firms must put as much emphasis on the quality of their content as they do on the ways they take it to market.

Still not convinced about the limitations of a marketing-centric approach to thought leadership? Let's examine them.

Dimension	Marketing-Centric Mindset	Content-Centric Mindset
Role of thought leadership content	Creating demand (marketing and sales programs)	Creating demand and supply (marketing, sales, services and service approaches)
Orientation	Extensive marketing will overcome shortcomings in substance	Extensive marketing can't overcome substance shortcomings. Only shoring up substance can.
Budget priorities	Majority on marketing Minority on content	Majority on content Minority on marketing
Depth	Low number of competing and viable solutions	Significant number of competing and viable solutions
Reporting relationship	Believes content (e.g., thought leadership research) should report to marketing	Content won't report to marketing. Will only report to the CEO
Role of thought leadership	Confirm existing approaches	Create new approaches
Importance of content development skills	Low	High
Importance of content marketing skills	High	Low
Content quality standards	Few (if any) and not captured or shared	Many, captured, shared and enforced
Messaging preferences	Memorable sound bites	Game-changing ideas that shatter conventional wisdom.

How does a marketing-centric approach to thought leadership undermine a firm that wants to compete on the basis of thought leadership? In my career, I've seen it play out in several ways.

First, a marketing-centric mindset will view thought leadership as a marketing game — i.e., the creation of content to generate market awareness, leads and revenue. It won't, however, see thought leadership as also being about using that content to create new service approaches or new services.

Second, when confronted with weak campaign results, people with a marketing-centric mindset will say the solution is simply more marketing: greater press outreach, more dollars invested in Google ads, more frequent social media posts and more throwing good money after bad. A content-centric mindset, in contrast, would examine flaws in the content and try to fix them quickly. For example, are our case studies strong enough? Do they cite large and tangible benefits like revenue and cost improvements? If not, where can we quickly find stories that do?

Third, a marketing-centric approach will favor spending more of the thought leadership budget on marketing and less of it on content development. People with a content-centric approach realize that generating great content often requires spending more on developing that content (especially through primary, best-practice research) than spending on marketing. Those with a content-centric mindset also believe that great content, with some marketing, will be shared, liked and in general spread to a much greater extent than poor or average content.

The fourth difference between marketing- and content-centric thought leadership approaches can be found in company reporting relationships. Content-centric companies best operate when the thought leadership research function reports above marketing to the top of the company. This saves content from being subservient to marketing's demands. It also increases the chances that thought leadership content is used for updating services and creating new ones, not just giving marketers more material.

Reengineering guru Mike Hammer would never have agreed to report to the head of marketing at CSC Index. If he had to answer to anyone — and he wasn't an employee of the firm (he was president of his own education firm and a partner with CSC Index in a joint venture) — it would be to CSC Index CEO Jim Champy.

The fifth difference in the marketing-centric approach is that it can skimp on articulating quality standards. Content-centric firms are more likely to have quality standards for content, and they're more likely to adhere to them. They are just more religious about the need to have groundbreaking solutions to customer problems — solutions supported by real evidence that they work.

Marketing- and content-centric mindsets also take different approaches to thought leadership training. Marketing-centric firms favor training in social media marketing, event management, public speaking skills and other marketing tasks. Content-centric firms opt for learning new skills in designing and analyzing primary research, argument development and other capabilities that are crucial to improving ideas.

Finally, both camps also have different preferences in messaging. Marketing-centric people often push for memorable soundbites — crafty one-liners — that can get immediate attention in a marketplace burgeoning with competing messages. In comparison, content-centric people are enamored with elegant, game-changing ideas that can't be adequately boiled down to a sentence or paragraph. Those ideas might require 1,000 words, maybe 10,000, for their beauty to be recognized.

A marketing-centric view of thought leadership is guaranteed to confine a company to thought *followership* status, not thought *leadership*. To win on the basis of thought leadership, companies must have a *content-centric* mindset and take a *content-centric* approach.

So now that we've put compelling content at the center of your thought leadership solar system — the star around which everything else that you do will revolve — let's dive into the source of content that has propelled many rising experts into world renowned thought leaders. That source is primary research. The next chapter is devoted to this topic.

CHAPTER 5

CONDUCTING PRIMARY RESEARCH TO PRODUCE BLOCKBUSTER CONCEPTS

+ + + + + + + +

THE PREVIOUS CHAPTER DISCUSSED how great content, more than great marketing, is at the center of a company's ability to compete on thought leadership.

This chapter will focus on one of the generators of great content: primary research. Such content comes from studying a number of companies — clients and other organizations — that have grappled with the business problem that is the topic of the research. As I'll explain, the most compelling thought leadership research I've seen and have conducted compares two groups: the companies that are the most effective in addressing the business problem at hand, and the companies that are least effective. (Chapter 6 will dive into what I call field-experience-based content. This content is *not* based on such primary research, but rather on the work that a company has done with its own clients.)

PRIMARY RESEARCH: SEED CAPITAL OF BLOCKBUSTER CONCEPTS

The holy grail of thought leadership is having a new and better way of solving a complex and critical business problem in the marketplace. Solutions to these problems can command premium prices. If explained well, supported with real evidence and marketed well enough to reach companies that have the problem themselves, those solutions can attract adherents rapidly. The firms behind those solutions can also grow rapidly — often far faster than they ever imagined.

Primary research has been behind many blockbuster concepts, including reengineering, disruptive innovation and blue ocean strategy. Well-designed and well-executed primary research became the underpinning of these breakthrough ideas, which in turn fueled the fortunes of the companies that presented those ideas. Discovering patterns in the ways in which multiple organizations solve a complex problem is one of the most enjoyable moments one can have in thought leadership. It's when you realize you are onto something very big — if you are the first to dissect the problem and solution well, codify it so that it can be marketed as a service and delivered as a repeatable process, and then be the first to bring it to the audience that needs it.

Between 1988 and 1995, CSC Index developed and marketed a superior approach to solving productivity problems in Fortune 500 companies — business reengineering. Its revenue rocketed fivefold, from $40 million to $200 million.

It wasn't by accident. It wasn't because of a single white paper, one or more glossy thought leadership journals, a memorable conference speech or a bestselling book. Yes, those and much more were part of the firm's marketing mix. But it was the ideas behind it all that fueled enormous client interest and great revenue growth. The concept of reengineering forever changed how companies improved key business processes.

That content came from primary research, through a research company that CSC Index co-owned with Hammer for a decade, called PRISM (for Partnership for Research in Information Systems Management). Their research process involved deep case studies done on what PRISM sponsors (more than 100 big companies at its peak) were doing on the topics at hand.

Multiple PRISM studies from 1988 to 1993 helped Hammer and CSC Index identify and develop their reengineering concept. Through their qualitative research, they determined what separated the companies with the greatest returns on information technology from the companies with the smallest returns. The "leaders" who reaped the greatest value redesigned the work across functional siloes, rather than automating the siloes and creating islands of automation, they found. They called what the leaders did reengineering, and then created a consulting practice around it.

Hammer and his research team spotted the practice across dozens of best-practice companies. They then coined a label for the practice

— redesigning business processes across functional silos — which was "business reengineering." I remember Hammer telling one reporter after the reengineering craze was in full motion: "I didn't invent reengineering. I discovered it."

Those seven words speak volumes about how to conduct thought leadership research. Hammer and the CSC Index research team "discovered" best practices in the application of information technology in the PRISM thought leadership research program. His thought leadership research method has been repeated numerous times over the last 30 years, by many more companies, and with varying degrees of success. The concept of reengineering was among the biggest of them.

HOW *NOT* TO CONDUCT THOUGHT LEADERSHIP RESEARCH

Perhaps one of the most important things to understand about thought leadership research is that it's *not* market research. I've seen this mistake made several times, and I think I know why: They're both forms of customer research. Yet they have very different goals, and very different approaches. Let's start with market research.

The goal of market research is to help a company improve its current products or services, support those offerings, create marketplace messages to generate interest in them, and/or identify new product or service needs. Market research may seek to find out whether customers like a company and its products, and whether some aspects of customers' lives have been improved because of it. This is vital research, for sure.

Thought leadership research, however, is different. The goal of thought leadership research should be to identify the most successful approaches to solving a client problem. Those problems could be ones that the company addresses currently, or ones it wants to address in the future. Thought leadership research may look at how customers are solving the problem themselves, or how other organizations are helping them solve those problems.

The differences between market research and thought leadership research are subtle but profound. A real example will help explain them. An architecture firm came to me a few years ago after conducting rigorous research on the impact of a type of building it had designed for several clients. It underwrote post-occupancy studies to see if those buildings had produced the type of impacts that its clients (colleges and universities) hoped for. Those impacts included greater collaboration among building visitors (professors and students), more students using the building and more students enrolling at the colleges, in part because the buildings looked like great places to study, do lab work and congregate with professors and other students.

This was an excellent piece of market research that the architecture firm had conducted on its work: the impact for its higher education institution clients. This was akin to an automaker, personal care company or barbecue grill manufacturer fielding a customer satisfaction study. No doubt, it helped the architecture firm get more work. But wasn't thought leadership research.

Had the architecture firm done thought leadership research on the client problem its services addressed — how to design a certain type of campus building for maximum teaching and learning impact — it would have included but looked far beyond its client base. Most important, it would have studied colleges and universities that *hadn't* used its design services, including those that used other architects to design their buildings. (By the way, the field of inquiry would have included institutions that designed these buildings without the help of an architecture firm.)

The architecture firm's thought leadership research question would have been this: What are the design principles behind campus buildings that have had the greatest impact at universities around the world? That's a far cry from the market research question: "What kind of impact have our university clients seen from the buildings we designed for them?"

Hammer and his research team from CSC Index weren't studying how the consulting firm had improved its clients' businesses or the quality of its services. They had a much grander agenda: finding, deciphering and then codifying the most effective ways big companies improved how they generated demand (marketing, sales), satisfied customers after their purchase, and produced and distributed their product and service offerings.

ROPING COMPANY EXPERTS INTO THOUGHT LEADERSHIP RESEARCH

It's no surprise that some of the biggest concepts in thought leadership over the last 30 years were created by small internal groups that didn't face the pressure of billable hours in their companies' mainstream businesses.

Where a company conducts its thought leadership research (e.g., in a protected think tank), and *how* (with or without the involvement of the firm's fee-generating professionals) can greatly affect the degree to which it embraces the concepts that come out of the research. B2B companies that compete on thought leadership but whose research isn't the principal revenue source need to think carefully about where they conduct their thought leadership research, and how they get others in the firm involved in it.

Too many B2B firms essentially outsource thought leadership research to a third party. In fact, a flock of firms have emerged over the last two decades that are in this very business: designing the study you want, putting a survey into the field, collecting and analyzing the data and writing your thought leadership report. They typically will also ask you to put their logo on the report next to yours, with the assertion that their brand has great value and that your research will be held in higher esteem if their brand logo is affixed to your study. Many B2B firms have bought into it.

I believe it's wrong-headed. It doesn't look good for your firm's brand message if it's outsourcing its ideas to a third party. If the content is compelling, who will be viewed as the thought leader from such research? The answer is the third-party firm whose name is on it, whose people designed the study, analyzed the data and wrote the report. That won't be your firm.

There's another problem with outsourcing your ideas to a third party that conducts thought leadership research for you: Your company's subject experts are not likely to get behind the study, even if it leads to the thought leadership version of an Einsteinian scientific discovery. Imagine if your great study hit the market, generated significant marketplace interest . . . but sparked little interest from the experts in your firm who ultimately need to incorporate the research insights into their selling and their work with clients. That study would be an orphan in your company, a strong but still unwanted piece of content.

And there's a related problem: Since you've outsourced your research to a third party, the "solution" to the problem formulated by your third-party researcher may not be something your firm practices. Your firm may not actually have the deep expertise that your big idea in the research report suggests it has. It's the concept car problem. You market an awe-inspiring futuristic automobile and consumers rush to car dealers to see it . . . only to be told no such car exists, now or possibly ever. It was just a concept.

With this in mind, the steps I provide in the next section are to reduce the risk of this scenario — i.e., of having even exceptional ideas unveiled by research to be rejected by colleagues who had no input into the research but are on the hook to deliver on the ideas.

THOUGHT LEADERSHIP RESEARCH: DOING IT RIGHT

The goal of thought leadership research should be to identify, understand and codify superior solutions to business problems — wherever you find those solutions, including outside your firm. How can you design thought leadership studies that achieve this lofty goal — and get buy-in from your entire organization? I've found that the following three things, if executed well, can lead to big ideas that an organization can get behind:

- Design the research with an inclusive team that goes narrow but deep, and seeks to break new ground.

- Gather both data and stories (especially stories) through old and new kinds of primary and secondary research — research that distinguishes what the most successful companies are doing differently.

- Get the company's experts involved in the analysis, but tee up a first-level analysis to optimize their time.

I'll illustrate these ideas through the steps that the leading Indian consulting and IT service company, Tata Consultancy Services, has used to power up its thought leadership research since 2010. TCS's market capitalization has increased from $25 billion in 2010 to more than $160 billion early in 2021.[59] Its revenue grew more than three-fold, to $22 billion, over that decade. Many factors are behind TCS's extraordinary success, but the company believes it has benefited greatly from increasing market recognition of its deep expertise in digital transformation. TCS studies on the topic have resulted in three articles in the most prestigious management publication in the world, *Harvard Business Review*, and opened up doors that have led to tens of millions of dollars for more client projects.

Research Design: Narrow and Inclusive

Since the goal of thought leadership research is to identify and codify superior approaches to solving complex business problems, the first step in designing a study is to define exactly which business problem to examine. In the crowded market of thought leadership studies, there's a good chance that many problems have already been studied by other organizations. In fact, a 2018 study of thought leadership marketers found that 75 percent of companies with at least 1,000 employees were conducting thought leadership research.[60]

To increase the chances that your thought leadership research will say something new and important, narrow the scope. With the limitations of time and budget, a yard wide and a mile deep is far better than a mile wide and a yard deep.

TCS learned this lesson over the last decade, when it made the commitment to invest in thought leadership research on digital transformation. The company realized at the outset that digital transformation was a very broad topic — so broad that it would be impossible to do justice to it through a single study. So it carved up this broad issue into narrow slices. Its first slice was on cloud computing (2012). It then published research later that year on mobile devices; big data and analytics software (2013); social media marketing (2013); digital corporate initiatives (2014); the Internet of Things (2015); artificial intelligence (2016); digital marketing (2019); digital ecosystems (2020); digital leadership (2021) and other topics. The research continues through this day.

Even within a narrow topic, the research team often must narrow the inquiry even further. Take big data. Large companies collect all sorts of data — about customers, suppliers, employees, competitors, etc. In its big data study, TCS decided to focus on *customer* data — largely because understanding how other companies collect, process and use their customer data had a far greater impact on revenue than other types of data. TCS also used another scoping mechanism for that study and for every other study its thought leadership institute conducted: It explored what a dozen or so industries were doing on the topic — not just any one industry and not just any size company. Typically, the companies TCS studied had at least $1 billion in revenue. Over the decade, this relentless focus has helped TCS codify its expertise and publish deeper-by-the-year research on these industries.

Scoping a topic tightly is also done better if it's a team exercise — involving researchers, thought leadership marketers and company thought leaders (current and aspiring). Including a company's subject experts in thought leadership research is crucial to success, if you define success as having the firm fully capitalize on the concepts the research unveils. This is taking an *inclusive* approach to research design and analysis. The idea comes from Serge Perignon, head of TCS's Thought Leadership Institute and a client of mine since 2011.

He has led more than a dozen thought leadership studies in the last decade, and helped TCS raise its image as an expert in digital strategy and implementation. Perignon uses an inclusive approach in every study. It is where the magic begins in great thought leadership research.

Having one overarching research question is also crucial in designing thought leadership studies that will have resonance in the marketplace and within the company. Any study's findings should be able to answer one core question. That's another mechanism for keeping the scope of thought leadership narrow while going deep. The core question that Mike Hammer and CSC Index had for that first study that identified the reengineering trend was this: How do the best companies use information technology differently than other companies? For TCS's latest study (on digital leadership strategies, launched in 2021), the core question was this: Are the most successful companies of the last decade focusing their digital initiatives this decade more on *innovation* (radically changing what they do) or on *optimization* (improving on processes and services already in place)?

After determining your overarching research question, the next step is to break it down into sub-questions, each of which should have an initial hypothesis about what you and your research team (and your company's other experts on the topic) believe the study is likely to find. The best way we've broken an overarching topic into its subcomponents is through a problem-solution framework:

1. What is the specific problem of the target audience?

2. How do we believe most of them have been trying to solve it, and why are they falling short?

3. How do we believe the most successful companies are solving the problem?

4. What are the key barriers to adopting the superior solution, and how did the best companies overcome them?

Remember that the role of thought leadership research is to produce new insights, not confirm existing ones. This means that going into a study, your firm will know much more about items Nos. 1 and 2 than it will know about Nos. 3 and 4. Even though you hope you'll learn great new things about Nos. 3 and 4, you'll still need to create initial hypotheses to guide the questions you ask in a survey, your interviews with companies and other research streams.

You may need to abandon your initial hypotheses when your data comes in about what the most successful companies in addressing the problem are doing differently than the rest. In fact, you should *want* to abandon your initial hypotheses because they are likely to reflect conventional thinking about the issue. You want to use the research process to uncover entirely new things. This is when a long, rigorous thought leadership research process can generate new and important insights.

In its 2015 study on the Internet of Things, the TCS research team (including the TCS consultants who helped analyze the data) stepped back from their findings to make an important observation. They saw that many companies were installing digital sensors in their products and other digital devices in the places they did business with customers (e.g., bank branches, amusement parks, stores, etc.). However, those that got the greatest value from this technology were not doing it to "spy" on customers or sell them more things. No — they were using IoT technology to monitor how well their products and places were performing for customers "in the field." Once they were able to monitor their products and services, they were able to improve or fix them much faster, and thus please customers faster.

This was a revelation: Use IoT to improve your company's performance for customers. Top-tier media treated it as such. Here's how *Fortune* magazine's then-editor-in-chief Alan Murray responded to the TCS research in his newsletter to magazine subscribers: "I've now read [the study] and recommend it to everyone interested in the subject — which should include anyone running a bigger-than-a-breadbox business."

Doing all this work in research design might seem onerous and unnecessary, but it's essential. This may sound like a ton of work you must do long before your research team conducts a single interview or fields a single survey. Indeed, it is! But it's a thorough and inclusive process that will send a thought leadership study going in a productive direction, one that we've found to reap dividends in the marketplace.

It's no surprise that this research design phase can take 25 to 40 percent of the entire time it takes to execute a thought leadership research study. But it can be worth it, because research teams often don't know right away what they should be seeking. One note: Such an inclusive approach can make it difficult to do narrow but deep research if the inclusivity is too broad — that is, you get the input of dozens of people in your firm on what topic to explore. TCS has guarded against this by limiting its research design input to no more than six to eight people per study.

The next two elements are just as important.

Gathering Stats and Stories That Distinguish the Best from the Rest

Statistics are great, but stories are better. By stories, I mean case examples of companies that solved a problem along the lines you prescribe and got outsized benefits from solving it your way. Your clients relate to stories of how other companies solved complex business problems. It makes those problems appear solvable. It gives your clients reassurance that (following your approach) their problems can be solved, that they aren't being hustled into a solution.

And not just stories that illustrate the statistics — the two-sentence anecdotes that you glean from secondary research will be a break for readers weary from reading percentage after percentage. You need stories that make the business problem and focus of your research come to life, by showing how the most successful companies are solving the problem and where the less successful companies are missing the boat.

The case studies have been a core element of TCS's thought leadership research reports. In the last decade, they included how the Associated Press news service was using AI to write data-driven business and sports articles; how Microsoft was using AI to identify and ward off cyber hackers; how HP eliminated customers' worries about running out of printer ink (through sensors in HP printers that triggered purchases when ink levels were low); how General Electric monitored its aircraft engines to help airlines maintain them and fly their planes more fuel-efficiently; and many more. These case examples brought TCS's extensive research to life.

Inclusive Analysis Teams

After a research team has collected copious amounts of data from surveys and case interviews, the first thing it *shouldn't* do is go off to a retreat, analyze the data and hand their findings on a silver platter to the firm's experts. You might think you're doing your subject matter experts a favor by telling them the study's big findings. But you're not. If you tell them what it all means, they are not likely to be nearly as passionate about the findings as you are — no matter how counterintuitive and surprising your findings may be.

Your company's subject experts are the ones that clients and prospective clients want to speak with when the research is in the marketplace — not the research team. Clients want to talk to the people in a B2B firm who can help them adopt the solutions. If your SMEs didn't help come up with the research findings, they are far less likely to want to discuss them with potential and current clients.

It's not just because of the "not invented here" syndrome, although that can be a factor. It's because your subject experts are not likely to feel secure in talking about the research findings.

If you get your subject experts involved in analyzing the data and helping "connect the dots," they are more far more likely to see themselves as the thought leaders on the research and take it to the market. You want to not only develop thought-leading insights through thought leadership research; you also want to help develop thought leaders themselves.

MAKING SURE THE RIGHT SKILLS ARE ON THE ANALYSIS TEAM

Two people could look at the same body of primary research and field experience and come up with quite different conclusions about what the best practices are. If one of them is off the charts in the three skills below and the other is so-so, it understandably makes a huge difference:

- **Pattern recognition:** connecting the dots, so to say. This is where creativity is most useful.

- **Analytical ability:** rejecting conventional wisdom and getting to the root of success and failure, in the continual questioning of "why" — why some people/companies are far better than others at solving some business problem.

- **Communication:** explaining complex issues clearly and compellingly, with concepts and language that any person in business (including top management) can understand.

The people who a company puts on its thought leadership research teams matter greatly. Team members, as a whole, need to bring deep analytical, creative and communication skills. And they need to work extremely well together — drawing out, not discouraging, nascent ideas that have promise.

However, one person ultimately has to be "the straw that stirs the drink" — the person whose view ultimately determines the diagnosis of and solution to the topic at hand. There's much to be learned here from other creative professions. "Godfather" movie director Francis Ford Coppola drove the numerous daily decisions he had to make on movie sets from a unifying theme. "A director is asked a thousand questions a day," he told a trade publication, "so if you have a single theme unifying your movie, you can deal with all the details."[61] For Coppola, the theme of "The Godfather" series was succession. For "Apocalypse Now," it was morality.

As the illustrious film and play director Mike Nichols once said, "One person can't make a movie. But it's necessary that all the decisions . . . come from one mind." This rings true in thought leadership content.

To be sure, analyzing volumes of research data can take a long time. SMEs often don't have the time; they expect the research team to do it. But this is where the inclusive research process must be used.

The research team should develop what we call a "first-level" analysis of the findings. It should then label it that way with the SMEs and get them involved in subsequent rounds of analysis that unearth more insights from the data.

This is inclusive thought leadership research at its best. It greatly increases the chances that big ideas happen, and that a company's thought leaders take strong credit for them and get fully behind them.

CHAPTER 6

DEVELOPING EXCEPTIONAL FIELD EXPERIENCE-BASED CONTENT

+   +   +   +   +   +   +   +

I SHOWED IN THE PREVIOUS chapter the times when organizations need primary research in thought leadership: When they need to develop new solutions to the customer problems they choose to address. Studying what the best organizations do differently than the rest on an issue is the process by which groundbreaking ideas can be found.

But not every piece of content that a firm develops needs a study behind it. As I said in Chapter 4, you need primary research if your firm's solution is not novel or superior.

However, when your firm has a novel solution to a client problem and lots of evidence from client projects that it works very well, then you can draw on a different content source: your firm's field experience.

In this chapter, I'll explain how to develop compelling field-experience-based content. The key tool is one that I call the problem/solution outline. Think of it as a template to guide your content developers and subject experts as they collaborate on a piece of content and capture what's inside their heads.

The key skill in turning field experience into a powerful point of view is not what many people think it is — great writing skills. That is important, for sure. But a far more crucial skill — and also far harder to find — is one I call *argument development*. From our two studies with Rattleback since 2018 on thought leadership practices in B2B companies, we've seen that no more than one out of eight firms have that skill. And even among the most effective firms at thought leadership, only a quarter said argument development is a core skill at their firm.

Let's look at this and other skills for mastering experience-based thought leadership content. But first, I'll explain what I've found to be the biggest misconception about it.

HOW *NOT* TO CAPTURE FIELD EXPERIENCE

Field-experience-based thought leadership content will ultimately show up in articles, blog posts, conference presentations and white papers. Sometimes a firm's client experience is so vast and rich that it can turn it into a book.

But the biggest mistake companies make when they're trying to capture their unique, field-tested client work is thinking that *writing* articles, blog posts, conference presentations and white papers should *start* the process. They see the process as a prose-making process — i.e., collecting the thoughts of the subject experts whose bylines will go on the content and turning them into cogent sentences and paragraphs. They skip the most important step: creating a compelling argument first. Writing prose is a highly inefficient and usually ineffective way to do that.

The result: They dive into these "writing" projects with gusto, before they've fully developed their argument. That's a recipe for tremendous frustration and precious lost time.

The writing in the best books, presentations and articles is like the finish work on a gorgeous building. But it's the architect who designed the concept and created the blueprints. True thought leadership has the solid foundation of a bulletproof argument, supported by strong walls of experience, data and logic.

Take, for example, the book that pricing consultancy Simon-Kucher & Partners' Madhavan Ramanujam and Georg Tacke published in 2016, *Monetizing Innovation*. It was based on the firm's years of client work with such companies as Porsche, LinkedIn, Swarovski and Dräger Safety.[62] The book drew a tiny bit on the Germany-based consultancy's survey research on pricing over the years. But it was based far more on its 30-plus years of client field experience — hundreds of consulting projects for companies around the world since it was founded in 1985 by business professor Hermann Simon and his two doctoral students.

Many companies, however, still take a writing approach to producing articles, blog posts, presentations and white papers: talk to a subject expert or two (or more), do some desk research, ghostwrite a first draft, get input, finalize and publish. (Books, of course, are a lot more complex.) In fact, at the start of my career in thought leadership, I did it this way. It was inefficient, time-consuming and ego-crushing.

Tom Waite, my boss at CSC Index, had a print publication (*Indications*) that went out every few months. Each article was to be a weighty treatment on a topic for the firm's target clients: chief information officers at large companies. My process of distilling the expertise of the firm's super-smart consultants into 2,000 words or so was the process I used in journalism: Schedule time in their busy days (when they were at one of the firm's offices rather than travelling to clients), discuss the topic they had in mind for an hour or so, read my copious notes from that conversation, and review slides they may have had, a speech they may have given or even some bullet-points they may have scribbled on a piece of paper before we sat down.

Believing that since they were paid thousands of dollars a day to give clients advice on how to manage the IT function, I figured that I merely needed to write what they said — to convert often rambling and underdeveloped thoughts into prose. Then, after multiple revisions based on their feedback, I would deliver a final draft weeks or sometimes months later.

That seemed like a good process — until the consultant-authors and I were into revision No. 10 (or sometimes more). That was tiresome enough; all parties were weary after revisiting the same ideas time and again, making adjustments to clarify fuzzy thoughts or adding examples to bolster assertions. More than occasionally a consultant sent a revision to me with a message to the effect of "I think we need to take a very different approach to this article," or "I think we haven't addressed the core issue," or "I think we're addressing the wrong core issue; it's something else."

In papers like these — and there were far too many of them — neither they nor I was happy with the product. Ironically, they told me the prose was good. It was clear enough and an easy read. The issue was that the thinking — the ideas conveyed by the prose — wasn't entirely new. And when the ideas *were* new, they typically weren't convincing. That's because the authors lacked evidence to convince readers the problem was serious enough. Other times, authors didn't have enough evidence to show their recommendations had actually improved their clients' businesses.

This approach to capturing a firm's field experience is driven by prose production: writing, and writing, and writing some more before some authors say, "Yep, this is great."

I never liked the result, even if the authors did. And sometimes they didn't either. Unwittingly, we both had used the writing process to drive their thinking and codify their expertise. More times than not, that was a highly ineffective and inefficient process.

I had to come up with a better process, I felt, or I would hate my job and wish I had stayed in business journalism. The consultants whose ideas I had turned into prose were not unhappy . . . in fact, they thought I had helped them a lot. But I wasn't satisfied with the results because the outcomes weren't stellar by *my* criteria for compelling content. In many cases, I had greater ambitions than they had for their content.

I realized that we needed a better way. The way I chose was to first help them develop their thinking — shaping their argument about a client problem they wanted to offer advice on, and what they thought was a better way to solve it. I began to recognize that the core skill of thought leadership content development is argument shaping, not prose writing.

This process starts with what I call a foundational point of view (PoV). You can think of it as a firm's deep treatment on a topic — its profound examination on how to solve a key client problem. And the process for doing a foundational PoV puts argument-shaping — not prose-writing — at the center.

But a great foundational PoV will be the wellspring for all the thought leadership content that comes after it. It will make that content more bulletproof and compelling, and far easier to communicate.

DEVELOPING THE FOUNDATIONAL POINT OF VIEW

The process to create a foundational PoV takes longer, often considerably longer, than the process of taking input and quickly putting it into prose. It dives much deeper into the recesses of an issue. It requires far greater back-and-forth, probing and questioning between the authors and the person assigned to turn their expertise into a coherent argument. The first form it takes — a 5,000- to 10,000 -word (or even more) deep dive on an issue — is many more words than the typical blog post, article or even white paper that some B2B firms produce by the bushels.

Everyone who works with me to develop thought leadership content follows the process — the subject experts, the content developers who create the outlines and the writers who produce the prose according to detailed outlines.

My clients have found the returns on their foundational PoVs to be much greater. They have told me the benefits far outweigh the substantial time, mental rigor and effort they invested in them. FMG Leading said its foundational content on five topics was a key factor in tripling revenue between 2016 and 2020.) Not too long after the end of the process, they began to see why I call them "foundational": They become the source for derivative content — blog posts, articles, white papers, seminar and conference presentations, client briefings, and more.

More than they would have if they had relied on the prose-writing approach to developing thought leadership content, their derivative content was far more substantive and generated many more downloads than their prior content. Opinion article submissions carved out of foundational PoVs are much more likely to be accepted by top-tier publications. (For example, *Harvard Business Review* has accepted more than 70 percent of the articles I have helped clients develop through this process, more than 40 in all. That compares with *HBR*'s overall acceptance rate of unsolicited articles of less than 5 percent).[63]

To be sure, a foundational PoV is not the only way to help experts codify their expertise on solving a client problem. But it's the way I've seen work best. It results in deep, focused, rigorous content — content that persuades, content that has a better chance of changing opinions of even the most sophisticated readers about how to solve a complex business problem. It helps firms reduce the chances of producing shallow, unpersuasive content that can actually hurt their brands, according to research that we and others have done.

Let's next examine how to develop these foundational PoVs. Keep in mind that you *do not* need to know everything that your firm's SMEs know. But to master this process, you *do* need to become an expert in how to develop compelling arguments — on any topic. The key element of this process is a structured outline — what I call the problem/solution outline.

THE PROBLEM/SOLUTION ARGUMENT STRUCTURE

As I mentioned before, the best-designed homes and buildings were designed by architects. They didn't result just because building contractors started to create foundations, build walls and floors, construct roofs, and so on. And the best of the best had architects who worked well with their clients to understand what problems they wanted the building to solve.

The same principle applies to thought leadership content based on a firm or individual's experience with clients: Content developers need to work with the authors to help construct their argument. And every argument in thought leadership should be about a superior way to solve a complex problem of the target audience. We have found that a simple — but not simplistic — six-part argument structure works the best:

Problem/Solution Argument Structure
I. **Problem establishment:** Core problem, problem owner, and problem severity articulation
II. **Conventional solution review:** Problem dissection; why other solutions fall short
III. **New solution summary:** How it's different, benefits to those that have adopted it (high level)
IV. **New solution explication:** Steps to adopt it, and benefits and beneficiaries for those that do (in detail)
V. **Adoption barriers resolution:** How to overcome the major obstacles in adopting the new solution
VI. **First steps to solution:** How problem owners can determine whether and when they need to adopt the new solution, and first steps to take

Let's examine each piece.

Problem Establishment: Proving It's Real, and for Whom

The first part of every expert's argument about a better solution must be about "a solution to what"? Exactly what is the problem that the expert is pointing to? And who exactly has that problem? How do we truly know they have it?

A countless number of articles meant to sell you a new solution begin by failing to adequately explain how and why a problem affects you. Some go quickly into the solution (perhaps thinking that everyone knows about the problem). Others don't indicate who has the problem. Take an article that begins this way: "Executive teams are often misaligned on strategy. This is not optimal, and it needs to be solved." (I made that one up.) What members of executive teams? Most executive teams? What does "misaligned on strategy" mean? That they don't have the same understanding of it? They do, but they don't agree on it? And if so, what's the ultimate problem with that — that they don't agree on the strategy? How does that ultimately affect the direction, revenue and profit of their company?

Every problem statement must specify precisely what the problem is, who has it and the ultimate effect of not solving it well or at all, especially in dollars-and-cents terms. Problem statements that fall short on those counts are fuzzy. Your thought leadership content won't be read if it's plagued by fuzzy problem statements.

The issue with an imprecise or altogether-missing problem statement is that the audience can't immediately relate to the content. They won't want to devote an hour or more to reading about a problem that they are not sure they even have. This won't fly in a world in which your target audience can search on Google and summon up 10 other articles in a second that might actually have a crisp problem statement. Many readers rightfully stop reading content with fuzzy problem statements. That is a shame if, in fact, the content eventually presents a novel solution with compelling case examples.

Here's an example of a better way to start an argument, by way of a 2017 paper by FMG Leading (a client of mine):

> The healthcare industry is undergoing a dramatic transformation, and needs highly effective physician leaders who can pull their organizations through it. Now more than ever, hospitals and other healthcare services enterprises need seasoned doctors who also have the well-honed managerial and leadership skills to run a business. Several studies show that clinicians with the right leadership skills are much better suited to direct enterprises providing high-quality yet cost-effective care than are administrative and business professionals. One of them, an analysis of the top 100 U.S. hospitals, found "the best-performing hospitals are led disproportionately by physicians."[64]
>
> Yet the industry has an acute shortage of physicians with the experience, skills, and capacity to lead effectively. Why has the industry failed in this respect, and how must it change the way it develops physician leaders? From 30 years of working with executives across industries — the majority from within healthcare — we have seen both the power of effective leadership and the costs of poor leadership. Those experiences have shown us what physicians need to become great leaders.[65]

This article sums up the problem early and clearly: Health systems need physicians with great management and leadership skills to help their organizations take on massive change. It provides evidence behind that statement — that the best-performing hospitals are managed more often by doctors. And the second paragraph hints at the problem behind the problem: a big shortfall of highly effective physician leaders.

If you can succinctly capture the problem in the world that you're writing about and — when it's an arguable problem — bring facts that show it's widespread, you have a very appealing worm on the hook to reel in a reader. But when your problem statement is missing or fuzzy, you have a hook without a worm or a hook with seaweed. You won't catch even a minnow.

Conventional Solution Review: Why Other Approaches Fall Short

Rarely is any firm the only one capable of solving an organization's problems; it's likely that many other solutions exist. And organizations might lean on their own in-house experts to solve their problems. You don't necessarily need a consultant to digitize your marketing if you have a tech expert on staff, or an outside law firm to protect the organization against an employee action if you have in-house counsel.

With thought leadership, nearly every time you are selling against other solutions. We all wish that weren't the case. But reality typically intrudes. You must make the reader understand that you are well familiar with other established solutions they're exploring or considering to solve their problem. That buys you more trust with your audience — that you feel their "pain" and how they've tried to reduce it, but without results.

But a caution here: You should avoid directly naming and knocking competitors in any of your messaging. Many buyers will see that as unseemly, as a gratuitous insult. You don't need to elevate your solution by denigrating others by name.

Instead, when you review the typical solutions, you should refer generally to them. As an example, say you have a new solution to finding exceptional talent. Rather than saying things like, "Candidates found through LinkedIn typically are misses rather than hits," you should say something different because it casts LinkedIn negatively and because it may very well be inaccurate. What if the reader has used LinkedIn and found great employees? So instead, if the problem statement is that recruitment through online sites like LinkedIn often involves phony credentials, I would phrase it something like this: "Looking for job candidates on sites that allow them to fill in their own job backgrounds with no verification can produce prospects whose backgrounds are bogus."

In other words, there's no need to denigrate LinkedIn. (By the way, I have no idea about its quality as a recruitment tool. I imagine it's a very crucial tool for many recruiters.)

The more you show about the shortcomings of the solutions you are selling against — and the greater proof you can bring that these shortcomings are real — the better you will convince your audience you know their pain point.

New Solution Summary: New Approach in Brief

This and the next piece of the problem/solution argument structure are the same thing: a description of the new solution that you will subsequently unpack for the audience. It helps to summarize the solution in a paragraph or two (or on one slide in a conference or webinar presentation) before diving deep into it. Because the solution part of your argument should constitute 40-50 percent of your total content, you will want to give your audience the juiciest details first. Otherwise, they may get lost when you begin explaining your solution in great detail.

With that in mind, your new solution summary should do the following:

- Explain either the steps or the key elements of your solution, captured in bullet points here or some other one-line form.

- Name drop: Mention the names of company examples you'll use to illustrate how others have used the solution.

- Show them the money: State the range of benefits that those companies have generated (e.g., "Streamlining supply chains this way helped Dell take 20 percent of the time out of its manufacturing process").

The third bullet is the most important, and I used Rod Tidwell's unforgettable line in the movie "Jerry Maguire" to sum it up. Just as the most memorable line from the movie was about the benefits Tidwell wanted his agent (played by Tom Cruise) to get in a new pro football contract, the place to show your reader the money is in your new solution summary.

New Solution Explication: The Approach in Detail

After giving the highlights of your novel solution and companies that benefited from it, you then have encouraged the reader to find out how they, too, could get such benefits. This will be the meat of your argument. Be forewarned that if you don't have real examples of companies that benefited mightily from solving the problem using your solution, you'll have very little to explain.

When you do have those examples, you will want to use them to illustrate the steps of your solution, or the key elements of it if you don't want to explain it as phases in a process. Those examples will serve two purposes: They'll show that your new solution actually works (remember the evidence requirement of thought leadership), and they'll turn what can be a dry and complex prescription for improvement into something exciting that will keep your audience engaged.

It is in this section that you'll want to pack in as many details as you can about the problem that your case examples faced (which will help confirm your upfront problem statement) and what was at risk to those companies before they solved it. Using real examples is a requirement here; do not rely on using fictitious or composite examples from several companies. You need to have most of your case examples name the companies involved, and preferably also name the people in those companies who helped solve the problem. This is where you will likely come across a big impediment: Clients who don't want to give your company a testimonial.

Using the right approach from the outset can help you overcome this resistance. The key is to tell these clients you don't want a testimonial at all. In fact, you want to make them the heroes of your content — and portray them as executives who solved a problem at their companies.

This way, you are favorably mentioning their companies as overcoming some key issue. And you are favorably mentioning your client executives as key to solving the issue. That is good for their company's public reputation, and for their careers.

I've convinced a number of my B2B clients' clients to be featured in thought leadership articles by selling their participation this way. But you will need to keep your own company's name out of the content — i.e., don't use phrases like, "We helped company XYZ. . ." Otherwise it sounds like you're taking credit for solving their problem.

The fact that your firm (and people in your firm) are authoring the article will strongly imply to readers that your firm was involved, because the details about companies and their people couldn't be gleaned otherwise.

Adoption Barriers Resolution: Overcoming the Implementation Hurdles

By this time in your content, you are near the last one-quarter of your argument. Your problem statement is clear, the flaws of conventional approaches to solving it are understood, and your new solution is laid out and seen to work splendidly. But you're not done. It's time to show that you deeply understand the challenges to implementing your solution.

In this section, you must show you know where your clients are likely to get hung up in trying to solve the problem your way. You must also demonstrate that you know how they can overcome those adoption barriers.

This section should feature three to five of your key adoption barriers, not all of them. This is your chance to show indirectly that your firm has done this work and knows what an organization will face in trying to adopt your approach. Importantly, you must explain how to overcome those key adoption barriers, and the best way to do that is with more real case examples.

In fact, returning to the case examples you used in the previous section will work best here because the reader will already be familiar with them. But you are not limited to those examples. Any example that shows how a company overcame the barriers will work.

First Steps to Solution: What to Do Tomorrow

The last piece in this six-part argument structure should give your audience hope and guidance on moving to your solution. One way to handle this is to have them self-diagnose whether their company has the problem you are pointing to. Another is to give them the first steps to solve the problem.

This piece of the argument structure should be brief. If readers have gotten this far through, that's a sign they're interested to learn more about your firm's services.

Now with those six pieces of a thought leadership argument in mind, the next step is not to start writing. Rather, it is to put your thinking into an outline that follows the six-point structure.

DEVELOPING THE ARGUMENT: STARTING WITH AN OUTLINE

Every foundational PoV should be scoped out using these six parts to structure the outline — both the initial outline (a very brief overview, maybe 1-2 pages, to get the overall logic in place) and then the final outline before the writing begins (a detailed outline of 10-20 pages or more, whose word count can often be longer than the prose that follows). What's more, at least three-quarters of the work involved to help an author or several authors codify their ideas into a highly compelling and well-written foundational PoV will be for argument development. No more than 25 percent of the time should go into writing the prose that follows a detailed outline.

Again, this is because the biggest factor behind a highly persuasive PoV is a powerful argument — one whose problem is highly relevant to the target audience; whose solution has been shown to work, and work well; whose logic is irrefutable; whose command of the topic is deep; and whose examination of how to solve the problem is extensive, not cursory.

Not as important, but still important, is how the argument is conveyed. This is the job of the prose writers: to not only convey the argument as laid out in the detailed outline, but also to convey it in as readable and enjoyable manner as possible. Powerful argument + elegant writing = compelling thoughts.

OUR PROCESS:
separating argument-making from prose-making

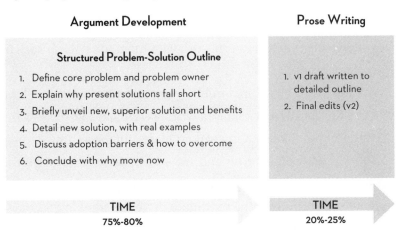

This process gets both the experts who will author a piece of content, and the content developers and writers they use, to stop using prose-writing to develop the thinking. To explain this, consider the degree to which an argument is compelling on a scale of 0 to 100 percent. Zero percent would mean the argument wouldn't convince anyone to any degree. The problem might be so muddy that no one can understand it. The solution to that muddy problem might either sound like you've heard it hundreds of times before — or something new but with zero evidence that it actually has worked. No real examples illustrate either the problem or the solution. There may not even be hypothetical examples. This would be an example of an argument that was on the left side of this spectrum.

In my experience, most thought leadership content projects begin with an expert's core argument being less than 50 percent developed

— i.e., without the logic, examples and other facts fully in place to constitute a powerful argument. (You might call such an argument "half-baked," but using that term with your experts probably wouldn't win any goodwill. In fact, it might mean an early project ending date!) Using the structured problem/solution outline with the subject experts means holding meetings, phone calls, email exchanges and other interchanges in which you work with them to establish each of the six elements of the outline.

Without such a structured outline, you and your authors will be relying on the ghostwriters' skills in writing clear and enjoyable prose, and on the authors' codification of their ideas. But the writing — draft v1, draft v2, draft v3, and on and on — will be used to drive the thinking. Of course, that is possible. But if the core argument is not strong, the issue of using the writing to drive the thinking becomes one of boredom, tedium and vested time that makes everybody very reluctant to change course.

It becomes boring to have to continue reading the same prose and seeing little advancement in the argument. It becomes tedious seeing baby steps made. And the vested issue is this: If you're 3,000 words into draft prose, you don't want the authors saying, "We need to start over because we think the argument is flawed."

Those are not words anyone wants to hear, even if the authors fault themselves.

The way to avoid that is not to use draft after draft of painstakingly written prose to push the authors' core ideas, but rather to use a structured outline to do that job. At the moment, after say v4 of a detailed outline, all parties agree that the argument is sound, evidence-laden, novel and proven — then is the time to write prose. But only then.

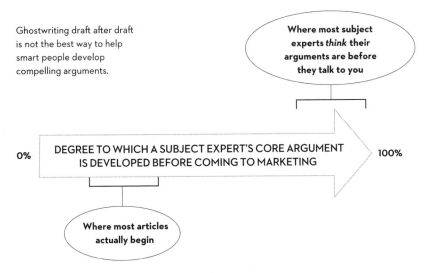

WHY PROSE ALONE USUALLY DOESN'T MAKE GOOD SAUSAGE

Ghostwriting draft after draft is not the best way to help smart people develop compelling arguments.

Where most subject experts *think* their arguments are before they talk to you

0%

DEGREE TO WHICH A SUBJECT EXPERT'S CORE ARGUMENT IS DEVELOPED BEFORE COMING TO MARKETING

100%

Where most articles actually begin

Putting the Outline Into Prose

When the authors of a foundational PoV and the people helping them construct it agree that a detailed outline is in great shape, then the next step is to write prose that follows that detailed outline. This is not the time to worry about length. Whether it takes 5,000, 10,000 or 20,000 words to make a bullet-proof argument is not important. The power of your argument — how novel the solution is, the number of real, identified case studies, and the size of the payoff for them — will overcome reader fatigue.

I've heard for 40 years that no one wants to read long articles. That's funny. Books are still selling, many of them in the 300 page or more range. Long articles in wonderfully written magazines like *The New Yorker* and *The Atlantic* can stretch on for 5,000 words, or even more. Readers are still reading long-form content.

For sure, readers won't read long-form content that is not stimulating, fact-filled and novel — or on unimportant topics. But a foundational PoV can be long — *if* it brings new ideas, is replete with real examples of companies that solve the problem at hand and addresses critical business topics.

Here's my rule of thumb when it comes to the length of a foundational point of view: Use the fewest number of words to make a weighty, irrefutable argument about a complex problem and a better way to solve it. That argument may require thousands of words — maybe 2,000, maybe 5,000, maybe 10,000. Maybe more. Stop only when you think nothing more needs to be said, proven or illustrated.

Once you have a compelling research study (as explained in Chapter 5) or an outstanding foundational PoV, the next step of course is to get your audience to read it. Unlike the 1989 baseball fantasy movie "Field of Dreams," in which a wonderful, dreamlike baseball field is carved out of an Iowa farm and attracts long-dead pros to the diamond, just because you built it doesn't mean your readers will necessarily flock to it magically. "If you build your thought leadership content, your audience won't necessarily come to it."

How to draw your target audience to compelling, thought-leading content is the topic of the next chapter.

PART IV

ATTRACTING THE RIGHT AUDIENCE TO YOUR CONTENT

MAKING BIG RIPPLES IN THE GLOBAL DIGITAL POND

+   +   +   +   +   +   +   +

SO YOU AND YOUR colleagues followed the advice in the previous three chapters and created an exceptional piece of content with an exceptional idea — something deep and substantive that will bolster your firm's reputation as the go-to problem solver and intrigue potential clients.

You based your content on primary research that divined the best ways to solve some client pain point. Or you based it on your company's own deep field experience with clients, through which it has developed a truly unique solution that has worked numerous times. Your point of view meets the tall tests of novelty, evidence, rigor, practicality and the other criteria that make powerful arguments powerful.

Congratulations! You are halfway up a steep mountain that aspiring thought leaders must climb before they start becoming recognized as thought leaders. The other half of your climb is getting your content in front of your target audience. If you fail to do that, you still will have created truly compelling content — but few will know about it other than your company's experts who are behind it, your firm's clients that have put your expertise to work and perhaps a few others with whom you have shared it. It's still unknown to the many organizations that would pay you handsomely to have you solve their complex organizational problems.

And while you may be an expert and be justifiably proud of that, you are not yet a thought leader — because a thought leader is renowned, and few know about you yet.

Our research on thought leadership practices supports this notion — that compelling content won't find a substantial audience on its own devices, and that great marketing is another piece of the thought leadership formula. Our 2020 research showed that the best companies at thought leadership said both exceptional content and effective marketing of such content were the top factors behind their most successful thought leadership campaigns between 2018 and 2020.

So how does an organization gain eminence after it's created a superior solution to a specific problem — expertise it has captured and codified in a research report, book, foundational PoV-type paper or some other weighty format? How does it gain the recognition it wants to gain, to generate the business that it wants to generate? That's the topic of this chapter. It's about attracting the right audience for your content.

Note that the "right" audience doesn't necessarily mean an audience in the millions. It just means reaching enough of the people who might need your services. For example, if an architecture and engineering firm wants to market its expertise in designing and building parking garages, its target audience goes little further than the executives and companies that need parking garages. That audience might include owners of buildings that need parking garages (stadiums, hotels, condos and apartments, etc.). And it might include other architecture firms hired to design those stadiums, hotels, condos and apartments but which lack parking garage design expertise.

Your audience may be only a few thousand people. Or, like Urban Science in its early years, when it sold expertise to automobile manufacturers on where to locate their dealerships, it may be even fewer — just the executives running dealer networks at automotive companies.

Or your audience could be much bigger — for example, tens or hundreds of thousands of executives to whom consulting and IT services companies sell their offerings: the so-called C-suite at billion-dollar-plus organizations. Companies like TCS and Accenture focus on that audience.

This is about audience-building: determining who and how many need to see an organization's expertise in order for that organization to achieve its revenue goals. Audience-building for consumer goods is about advertising (digital and non-digital), PR, experiential marketing, direct marketing, event sponsorships and other promotions that can reach millions or hundreds of millions of consumers.

In contrast, audience-building for thought leadership involves a very different set of marketing channels, although the consumer marketing channels could also be useful in amplifying how many people see the messages.

I'll explain two models for building an audience for thought leadership content. Both can be understood using a techie term: They are high-bandwidth, low-bias channels. That contrasts with the low-bandwidth, high-bias channels of traditional marketing.[66]

USING HIGH-BANDWIDTH, LOW-BIAS CHANNELS

Marketing products and services that solve well-understood needs — what I called image marketing in Chapter 1 — is done through marketing channels that are low bandwidth and high bias. By low bandwidth, I mean the medium doesn't allow the marketer to impart a great deal of information. A 20-second video ad, TV ad, radio spot, billboard, banner ad or print ad will do the trick. The message should be short, be clear and evoke a feeling. If the product or services need a little explaining, then you might need more than a short ad. Maybe an infomercial, or a website that goes in depth about a resort, or a travel brochure in the mail. Maybe an exhibit booth at a trade show, if the product is a little more complex.

These products and services need to be sold on a feature and function basis: What do the hotel rooms look like? What's nearby? Are there hiking trails? What do they look like? This is classic product marketing.

Whether it's image or product marketing, you know you are being marketed to. You know that these are ads, not unbiased news. Commercial breaks on TV are known as times to sell viewers something. This kind of marketing is high bias: You know the intent is to sell.

In contrast, thought leadership marketing is the exact opposite: It is high bandwidth and low bias. A foundational PoV paper that is

5,000 words long is a weighty piece of content. You won't "consume" it in 20 seconds like you would a Super Bowl ad for Cheetos. A conference presentation, whether seen at a hotel or on your computer, could take 45 minutes of your day. A book is a multiday commitment: hours of reading in solitude. Even a 500-word blog post can't be consumed in 20 seconds. We're talking minutes here.

These are all high-bandwidth marketing formats — lots of information imparted. Now comes the bias issue: They are not labeled or seen as blatantly promotional. They are educational. Have you ever picked up a business book because you thought you'd enjoy reading an ad for 10 hours? Of course not. Or do you sit in on conference presentations to be pitched a product or service? I doubt it. You are there to be educated on an issue of interest.

All thought leadership channels must be high bandwidth and low bias. That's because thought leadership content:

- Addresses complex problems with complex solutions.
- Sells offerings that are not impulse purchases; they have a long sales cycle.
- Must be seen as educational, not promotional.
- Must appeal to multiple people involved in the buying decision — a team rather than an individual.
- Requires exceptionally high degrees of trust because company performance and careers can be on the line.

Pre-web, these channels were mostly offline. (Email did exist before the web.) The channels were print publications delivered to an audience through the mail, in-person seminars and conferences, books printed on paper, phone calls, videoconferences (using high-bandwidth phone lines), etc.

Those activities were best done when they were orchestrated as a sequential "funnel" of activities. At the biggest end of the funnel you would stage audience-building activities aimed at your target audience. If your content was compelling enough, those activities then would attract a strong percentage of that audience into the funnel to find out more about the company and the services behind the thought leaders. Then a subset of those "tire-kickers" would get into a sales discussion.

Let's examine this — what I call the "phases of the funnel" model — more deeply.

PHASES OF THE FUNNEL: THE OLD AUDIENCE-BUILDING MODEL

The funnel model featured three types of activities, staged in phases:

- **Phase 1, awareness creation:** Getting your expertise in front of hundreds or thousands of prospects. This was done typically by sending articles, mailing whole publications, getting quoted in the press, placing opinion articles in the press or publishing books. It was one-directional communication.

- **Phase 2, relationship development:** Forming personal relationships with dozens of prospects who become aware of your expertise (without doing any selling yet). This was done by attending seminars and conferences at which the author of the book or article presented his or her ideas in an (ideally) compelling way. The presenter was then available after the presentation to talk with members of the audience, trade business cards and (if the speech was effective enough) talk business after returning to the office.

- **Phase 3, selling:** Converting a high proportion of prospects (with whom you've formed a personal relationship) to clients. The hope with the subsequent follow-up calls, of course, is to be asked to submit a proposal.

CSC Index mastered the sequential funnel. In awareness creation, in the late 1980s and early 1990s, we published two management journals, one for senior business executives (*Insights Quarterly)* and the other for chief information officers (*Indications*). We had three articles in the *Harvard Business Review* within five years (in 1988, 1990 and 1993), an annual survey of IT management issues that was a big generator of press mentions and three books — all U.S. bestsellers.

In relationship development, the company had a business unit (called Index Research & Advisory Services) that ran conferences at luxury resorts and other top hotels around the U.S. Those events attracted senior executives from large companies, who could hear Michael Hammer, Jim Champy, Michael Treacy (another ex-MIT professor, like Hammer) and other experts on reengineering, operational strategy, change management, emerging technologies and other key business topics. These weren't just any old corporate conferences. Many of the meetings were part of a half-dozen research programs that Index had launched, including the joint venture with Hammer. Those research programs were, in effect, externally funded thought leadership R&D. The program that Hammer and Index co-owned (PRISM) was where they identified the reengineering trend.

With these conference and research programs attracting hundreds of leaders of Fortune 500-size companies, they became great places for Index to develop client relationships. And many of those relationships turned into consulting projects, some a million dollars or more.

This is not an unusual model in the world of management consulting, IT services, software, financial services and accounting. Enterprise software companies such as SAP, Salesforce, Adobe and Oracle annually hold huge customer conferences. They are educational places to renew old client relationships and form new ones. But CSC Index's sequential thought leadership funnel was one of the most effective in the management consulting industry in the last 30 years.

Yet the internet, web videoconferencing and other technologies since the mid-1990s have revolutionized the ways in which thought leadership content can be shared, viewed and experienced. That has forced a rethinking of how to build audiences. While the sequential funnel hasn't gone away, because print publications and in-person events haven't gone away (although they've largely been on hiatus during the pandemic), we need another audience-building model for thought leadership that is far better suited to the online world.

THE AUDIENCE-BUILDING FORCES OF A DIGITAL ONLINE WORLD

When the web shifted the attention of buyers and sellers online, much awareness creation, relationship development and selling shifted online as well. Print publications had their online versions. Many seminars were done as webinars. And social media became a key channel in the old audience-building model in the first decade of the 21st century, as sites like LinkedIn, Twitter and Facebook helped marketers drive readers to online publications, webinars and websites.

But not all thought leadership audience-building was online. Until the pandemic, although print publications had been fewer and farther between, they still existed. Conference marketing was alive and well. Conventions held by the big enterprise software companies each attracted thousands of people. Salesperson visits were still common. The pandemic, however, accelerated the shift from analog to digital communications for an obvious reason: Most companies could no longer hold in-person business meetings.

Interactions around thought leadership content had to be digitally mediated. But a funny thing happened while many thought leadership marketers and the experts whom they promoted lamented their work-from-home existences: The advantages of online audience-building became much clearer.

Again, these changes and their benefits didn't appear suddenly during the pandemic. They have been in place for some time. The pandemic, however, accelerated them.

Access to Content

Pre-web, thought leadership marketing campaigns had expiration dates. The shelf life of the content was finite. A conference presentation was not available after the speech was given; it was only available to the people attending it. Printed management journals or individual articles would be placed on bookshelves or thrown away; even if they remained on shelves, their articles were hard to find (buried within binding). Same with books: placed on shelves and hard to comb through. Many thought leadership ideas died — or were left in the orphanage, and thus forgotten — shortly after birth. Readers' access to that content was only temporary, and according to the producer's schedule.

Now, with such content on a firm's website or available from Amazon, thought leadership ideas can live forever. Executives' ability to get that content is perpetual, and they can get it when *they* need it (rather than when the content producer makes it available).

Finding Accessible Content

The value of search engines like Google and Bing is simple: They can help your audience quickly access your thought leadership content — just by typing words into their search tool. The concepts you expressed in a newsletter, article, conference presentation, webinar or book three years ago are not lost forever or hard to find — if you put them online. When content is online, it lives forever and can be found easily, and you have put your audience in control of when they want to view it. They can do it on *their* schedule — i.e., anytime they want — and not on your schedule (the week you mailed out a newsletter, held a conference or had your book in bookstores).

Your audience is now in control of their process of finding expertise to solve their business problem.

Reach: From Limited to Global

This can actually work in the distinct favor not only of the audience, but also of the thought leadership marketers and the experts they are promoting. It's because when the target audience can access a firm's content online, that audience can be a global one. Anyone anywhere in the world can use a search engine and find your content (if they use the right search terms). Your reach is no longer just regional or local — or wherever you sent your publications, held your conferences and seminars, and so on.

Sharing's a Snap

But that's not the only advantage you gain when your audience-building is mediated through digital means. Given that your publication, article, webinar presentation, journal article, etc., is in digital form, your audience can share it with dozens or even hundreds of their colleagues with a few mouse clicks. Great content can go viral and travel farther and faster than it did when "going viral" meant copying articles on the company Xerox machine and putting them in office mailboxes.

These technologies force audience-builders to rethink the fundamentals of funnel campaigns. You can't only be thinking about phases, conducted sequentially, with awareness, relationship and prospect-conversion activities in each phase. In marketing our thought leadership content in the digital realm, we need a new construct that captures what's possible in that realm. I liken that construct to the ripples that a rock will make once thrown into a pond.

RIPPLES IN A POND: THE DIGITAL-AUDIENCE-BUILDING MODEL FOR THOUGHT LEADERSHIP

What I'm about to state is so obvious that it may sound insulting. I'll state it anyway because I think it's often overlooked when B2B companies design their thought leadership audience-building campaigns.

It's that the internet's vast web, as well as email systems (many of which reside on websites such as Yahoo.com and Google.com), have enabled people inside and outside organizations to send personal messages to one another across regions and times zones. Over the last 30 years, this has created a big universe by which anyone can reach out to everyone with a few clicks on their keyboard.

Remember what a company had to do to get its messages in front of other organizations around the world before we had interconnected email systems and the web. To travel from its origins on a typewriter keyboard to its target market required huge amounts of effort, time and money: direct mail content produced in mass quantities, mailed to physical addresses, run in print advertisements, and aired in radio and TV ads.

It's so effortless today that it's easy to forget how hard it was to send messages — thought leadership content or any other — just 30 years ago.

None of these activities was digitally connected to any other activities. The people in the audience that a marketer wanted to reach were not within that marketer's digital reach. Messages had to be printed for mailings, printed in publication ads, recorded for TV and radio spots, and so on. Using the geological analogy of bodies of water, the marketer and the marketer's audience resided in separate ponds, lakes, lagoons, coves, bays, rivers and other unconnected bodies of water. Their surrounding land masses themselves were unconnected to one another because of the biggest body of water: oceans.

Throw a rock in one pond or lake or lagoon, and the ripples don't go very far — within that pond, lake or lagoon. And for sure not outside that body of water.

The web and email systems have reshaped this fragmented landscape and connected these once-isolated bodies of water. This digitally connected universe has created one immense pond in which every marketer and every audience member with an internet connection can be reached.

This makes for a very different world for thought leadership marketers — the people in your company whom you've hired to get your content in front of your target audience. They need to fundamentally rethink how ideas travel, on their own and with the help of marketing. It doesn't mean abandoning the "phases of the funnel" model of audience building altogether. But it does mean supplementing it with another model.

I call that model the "ripples in the pond" model of audience-building. Drop a pebble in a pond and the water will ripple outward from that pebble. Throw a bigger rock into that pond — say, the size of a baseball — and bigger waves will ripple out. Pick up a small boulder with two hands, raise it over your head (but don't lose your grip!) and heave it into that pond and much bigger waves will ripple out.

THE "RIPPLES IN THE POND" APPROACH TO THOUGHT LEADERSHIP MARKETING

CHANNELS

PAID

- Advertising (search ads, banner ads, social media ads, etc.)
- Pay-for-play conference presentations
- Advertorials

EARNED

- Op-eds
- Books (issued by publishers)
- Conference speeches

SHARED

- Social media
- Organic search results

OWNED

- Company digital publications
- Email newsletters
- Company websites
- Company seminars and webinars

KEY PRINCIPLES OF AUDIENCE BUILDING

• **THE POWER OF EARNED:** For most firms, earned channels have much larger audiences and much more credibility than shared or owned channels

• **THE RIPPLE EFFECT OF QUALITY:** The higher the quality of thought leadership content, the more viewers it will attract

• **THE VALUE OF INCREASING OWNED:** Firms that increase viewers of owned channels (especially email subscribers) can rely less on earned and paid channels

• **USING EARNED AND PAID AS AUDIENCE BOOSTERS:** Earned and paid channels can enlarge the audience significantly

Consider the size of that rock that you toss into the pond to represent the weightiness of that thought leadership content that you've put on the internet. An inconsequential blog post is a pebble. A foundational PoV is a soccer-ball-sized rock. A primary research report or book is a boulder.

Now the number of words alone is not what accounts for the heft of the idea; it's the novelty of that idea's prescriptions, the case examples and other evidence that those prescriptions work, and other qualities that make for leading thoughts. In short, it's how compelling your PoV is.

The goal here, of course, is to make the waves — the power of your ideas — felt by the people swimming in your pond. They are your target audience. Those who are within 50 feet may feel those waves. But you want those who are hundreds of feet away — maybe a mile away (so now we're talking about a lake and not a pond!) — to know about your ideas. The farther you want your waves to ripple, the weightier your ideas will need to be, and the more content "rocks" you will have to throw in the water.

Dimensions of Comparison	Phases of the Funnel	Ripples in the Pond
Audience posture	Passive and reactive	Proactive and in control
Ease of locating content	Hard	Easy
Access to content	Temporary, and at producer's schedule	Perpetual, and at prospect's schedule
Reach	Local	Global
Ability to share	Difficult and time-consuming	Easy and fast
Engagement with content and people behind it (thought leaders)	Limited and periodic	Extensive and regular

Also realize that with search engines like Google and Bing, much of your better content will ripple out to your target audience and beyond without you having to do anything. Your content will be scanned by the web crawlers of Google, Bing and other search tools, and wind up in their search results. If more people link to your content, and your content signals to Google and Bing that it's high-quality, then your search rankings will rise.

Now consider adding another element to this metaphor: You can amplify each concentric circle that ripples out through four types of amplifiers, which extend out from your content in this order:

- Marketing channels that you *own* (your email contact list, your website, etc.).

- Marketing channels that you *share* but which are owned by others (search engines and social media sites such as LinkedIn, Twitter, YouTube and SlideShare).

- Marketing channels owned by others and in which your content must *earn* the right to appear (opinion sections of publications, management journals that run externally authored articles, conferences seeking outside speakers, etc.).

- Marketing channels that require you to *pay* to get the attention of your audience (search ads, banner ads, social media ads, conference presentations that require you to "pay to present," advertorials that require you to pay to publish, etc.).

For the typical B2B firm, its potential audience grows if it's willing to pay to reach that audience. Google processed nearly 12.7 billion search queries in January 2021 alone.[67] Nearly 2.5 billion people visit Facebook each month.[68] The amplifying channels that a firm owns — its email list, website, and so on — are the least expensive, of course. Getting content on shared media — i.e., social media — won't require you to pay those sites, but it will cost you a marketer's time. Note: That time can be a big investment in marketing labor — writing and responding to LinkedIn posts and comments, writing pithy Twitter tweets, etc.

The degree to which B2B companies use owned, shared, earned and paid channels to lure viewers to their content varies considerably. Our 2020 research showed that the best companies at thought leadership were far more likely to use all four types of channels than the least effective. In fact, the majority of the best firms used owned, shared, earned and paid channels in their most successful thought leadership campaigns between 2018 and 2020. In contrast, only a minority of the least effective firms used any of the four channels.

Digital Channels To Market	% of Most Effective Thought Leadership Marketers That Use Them	% of Least Effective Thought Leadership Marketers That Use Them
OWNED		
Email newsletters	63%	43%
Company webinars	19%	5%
Self-published white papers	51%	33%
SHARED		
Organic social media posts	54%	39%
LinkedIn and other third-party articles	54%	36%
Web videos on third-party sites, (e. g., YouTube, Vimeo, LinkedIn)	40%	29%
EARNED		
Opinion articles and third-party pubs	65%	47%
Press mentions	53%	32%
PAID		
Advertorials	61%	43%
Digital banner ads	7%	7%
Social media ads	49%	31%

Let's examine each ring. Generally speaking, the potential audiences that thought leadership marketers can reach get bigger as you get farther from the online thought leadership content that "splashes" in the digital pond. Tapping the channels in each ring can bring more viewers to your website, the epicenter of your digital universe of content.

Owned Media

If you have a company email newsletter with people who have signed up to subscribe to it, you have a regular and reliable channel to get your content to your target audience. This is a channel that you own, and which will have considerable value if you can grow it large enough with the right people as subscribers. "Right" largely means buyers and influencers on the purchase of your organization's services and products.

Company email newsletters, as conduits to thought leadership content, can be highly valuable channels. The technology research firm CB Insights has attracted more than 640,000 newsletter readers since it opened its doors in 2010. In 2016, the firm said its email open rate was 30 percent — about 50 percent higher than average.[69] That newsletter was the New York City firm's toehold into big tech and venture capital firms, each of which pays an average $70,000 annually for CB Insight's data.[70] The company says its revenue is in "the eight figures." Email marketing appears to be a place where many of CB Insights' client relationships have begun.

Shared Media

One of the most momentous changes in the world of business and consumer marketing began in the early 2000s when three of today's most dominant social media companies came to life: Facebook, LinkedIn and Twitter. They gave everyone an online website for connecting with friends, family members and colleagues with similar interests.

But for thought leadership marketers, these and other sites also provided the digital platform on which they could post their content, as well as short messages that would connect to content that resided on their website. Since then, the power of social media has been phenomenal — and horrifying at the same time — to watch. These sites have influenced political elections, helped armed groups to organize, gotten companies to admit to and back off from bad practices and policies, and helped "fake news" travel at the speed with which digital bits can traverse the internet.

I refer to the content and messages that any social media member can post as "shared media" because you don't own those sites; the owners of Facebook, LinkedIn and Twitter own them, and their management teams can determine whose content is appropriate or not to post. Nor are they "earned" media because they don't have editors who review your content and decide whether it should earn editorial space. And from the standpoint of thought leadership, you don't have to pay them to post your article. I can, and do, post articles on LinkedIn. I do post messages on Twitter and Facebook. And so do many other people who are trying to get attention for their expertise.

This is shared media, owned by others but open to you. Thus, you share their media to post your content. And by sharing your content on their sites, you can get it in front of a sizable audience — but only if you have a large number of Facebook, LinkedIn and Twitter connections.

Earned Media

One concentric ring beyond the "shared" ring is "earned" media. If a publication accepts your op-ed article, or a management journal runs your submitted piece, those are big wins in earned media. Their audiences view editorial content differently than they view advertorials or other content in which advertisers must pay to play. It is more likely to be read, and more likely to be seen as authoritative.

The audiences that the pages of *Harvard Business Review's* online edition (340,000 paid viewers alone), *Forbes.com* (132 million unique visitors worldwide) and the opinion sections of the digital editions of media like *The New York Times, Washington Post, Wall Street Journal, Financial Times* and *Fortune* are infinitely bigger than the audiences that the typical B2B company can attract to its website.

Experienced thought leadership marketers can spend significant money to get their company's experts' ideas into such vaunted places. Since 1998, my two firms have benefited from this spending, given that we have helped our clients develop, pitch and place more than 100 opinion articles in *HBR, Forbes, Sloan Management Review,* the *FT* and other leading publications. We helped one client (human capital strategy firm FMG Leading) get four articles into the digital version of *Harvard Business Review* from 2016 to 2018. Its *HBR* articles drove thousands of people in its target audience to the associated thought leadership content on the FMG Leading website.

Earned media such as this conveys much higher credibility than any firm's own website can convey with its thought leadership content. It's thought leadership's version of the Oscars, Emmys or Grammys ... a confirmation by discriminating judges that your ideas are worth something.

Earned media also lends authority to a thought leader's ideas in the conference world. Just about every conference uses keynote speakers who must be compensated for their services. These speakers are the epitome of earned content: They are getting paid by a marketing channel to present their ideas.

Paid Media

The outer ripple, to use my water metaphor, is paid digital media. The tactics in this channel for thought leadership marketers include search engine and social media ads, digital display/banner ads, advertorials and pay-for-play conferences that provide web archived video copies of speaker presentations.

The potential audiences here for your content are in the billions of people. But they can also cost you a lot of money. They add up quickly every time someone clicks on your Google ad or your Facebook or LinkedIn ad. Every person who clicks will ring up your bill.

MAKING BIG WAVES IN THE DIGITAL POND: THE STORY OF RAY DALIO

If you worked in the cloistered and clubby world of high finance, you likely know the name Ray Dalio. In 1975 he launched Bridgewater Associates, a Westport, Connecticut-based organization that has grown into the world's largest hedge fund firm, with $150 billion in assets. Dalio decided that he and his firm needed to be known not just for its financial heft but also for Dalio's management expertise. He published a book in 2017 titled *Principles: Life and Work*, which became a #1 *New York Times* bestseller. Dalio and his firm have actively marketed the book and its ideas through owned, shared, earned and paid media since then.

The impact has been remarkable. Research conducted in 2019 found that the press mentioned Dalio himself more times over a 12-month period than two other large asset management firms together: State Street Global Advisors and Natixis Investment Managers.[71]

Dalio first threw the ideas behind his book into the vast digital pond in 2011, with a 100-page PDF document on the Bridgewater website. That document, with 210 principles, had been downloaded more than three million times.[72]

Today, his shared media presence is wide. As of June 2021, Dalio had more than two million LinkedIn followers, 702,000 Twitter followers and 350,000 Facebook followers.[73] What's as notable as Dalio's followers is the number of times he answers their comments in those sites.

Looking at his comments in social media, I suspect Dalio realizes that his digital pond is one in which he must interact with his followers, and not simply preach at them as he would in the funnel model of thought leadership marketing.

MAKING WAVES IN YOUR POND

When I think in terms of digital channels for thought leadership, I find it more useful to think about the "ripples in the pond" model than the "phases in the funnel" construct. The "pond" metaphor reminds me that I can still make ripples with old content — if it's still relevant. Unlike news and magazine stories, most thought leadership content has a much longer shelf life. Thinking in terms of a pond rather than a funnel has prompted me to maintain a 20-year archive of my own articles about thought leadership on my Buday TLP website. Sometimes when I find I have written about the solution to a current market issue, I write a LinkedIn post with a link to an archived article, put a reference in our monthly email newsletter to it or Tweet a message with a link.

Your old thought leadership content, if it's on your website, never has to die. It isn't fated to live a life of neglect like the print articles or books that are read for a while and then gather dust on a bookshelf.

Or in the landfills where the many magazines and books that we no longer cherish end up.

KEY PRINCIPLES OF THE RIPPLES IN THE POND APPROACH

The key lessons to mastering the funnel approach to thought leadership were simple, yet hard to accomplish: Produce big research-based solutions to business problems; get them published as opinion and editorial articles in top-tier print journals; publish your own thought leadership journals and mail them to clients; write bestselling books; have great speakers from your firm present at leading conferences (the bestselling books will open those doors); and make sure your business development people are at those conferences to pick up the leads.

The biggest key to success in the digital pond is the same: great, research-based and evidence-based content trumps all. But the rest is a lot different:

- **Owned channels:** Make sure you have your own sizable digital platform of email newsletter subscribers, and content you can feed them regularly.

- **Shared channels:** Have a big presence (lots of followers and connections) in social media sites where your audience hangs out, and actively converse with them there.

- **Earned channels:** Publish and present in prestigious places — publications and conferences that revere thought leaders.

- **Paid channels:** Use these in times when you need to boost your digital viewership rapidly.

With those thoughts in mind, the most important principle to understand in a digital marketplace for thought leadership is this: Success depends not only on staging campaigns that bring new content to market (mastering a funnel with online *and* offline channels), but also on building audiences for both new and old-but-still-relevant content and making it ripple in the ever-growing digital pond.

Perhaps the biggest "Aha!" here — even for veteran thought leadership marketers — is reviving your old content through this digital pond. Look constantly for opportunities to showcase your old but still relevant solutions (to problems you wrote about in the past) when these problems become hot again.

Say that your law firm published a far-ranging and often-quoted article on your website five years ago about how to reduce the chances of getting hit with racial or gender discrimination lawsuits over allegedly unfair compensation practices. All of a sudden, a new lawsuit is filed by a senior Black female executive who just left her job at a highly admired mega-corporation, one considered to be a model for both financial performance and talent management. If you only followed the funnel model of thought leadership marketing, and you had no new content on this issue, you might be tempted to think, "Hey, that's an interesting news story," and leave it at that.

But if you also subscribed to the "ripples in pond" model, you would act very differently. You'd remember that your firm wrote a great, in-depth article on this very same topic five years ago. And then after making sure the article was still on your firm's website, you might have your web staff make a note of it on the home page. Then you should think through how you could create some ripples in the digital pond, using owned, shared, earned and paid wave-making tactics:

- **Owned:** Mention and link to your old content in your latest email newsletter and explain why your content is relevant now. Write a new blog post that points to the lawsuit and links to your old article.

- **Shared:** Write posts on LinkedIn, Twitter et al. that point to the lawsuit and then link to your old article (or your recent blog post). Also, get active in other people's LinkedIn posts about the lawsuit — by commenting on them, offering your solution and providing a link to the old article in which you elaborate on it.

- **Earned:** Scope out opportunities for submitting op-ed articles on the lawsuit to the right publications, and draw on your old content to formulate the "prescriptive" part of those op-eds. That old content of yours is the gift that keeps on giving; your PoV is already there. You might need to gather up some more recent examples when you do this. Use a sentence or word in that op-ed that links to your website content on the issue.

- **Paid:** If the above tactics don't generate sufficient traffic to your old content, consider paying for Google Ads, which can put you at the top of search results on this hot topic.

You may not have the immense resources that hedge fund billionaire Ray Dalio has to get a big audience to view your thought leadership content. But your company may not need even a fraction of his budget if you learn how to throw good-size rocks in the pond and use the owned, shared, earned and paid amplifiers to make bigger waves.

As viewers of thought leadership increasingly find and consume content on the web and through email, your thought leadership audience-building strategies and tactics must follow them. That's the reason why we all must think more and more in terms of the digital pond and less and less in terms of the traditional funnel.

Ultimately, the size of your owned channels, the extent to which you share your ideas in social media, your ability to generate earned media and the size of your digital advertising budget will determine how many people in your target audience view your thought leadership. Will it be 0.1 percent, 1 percent, 5 percent, 10 percent or more? That will depend on how well you use the four audience boosters of owned, earned, shared and paid media.

But let's not forget that the power of your ideas — how compelling they are to your target audience — plays a major role, too, in how far they travel. That's because your target audience is more likely to share exceptional content (through email or a link), "like" or "love" it on social media. They are also more likely to mention it in their own thought leadership content (ideally, with links to your content).

CHAPTER 8

TURNING WEB VISITORS INTO PRIME PROSPECTS: THE POWER OF THE VISUAL

+   +   +   +   +   +   +   +

WHEN YOU'VE BROUGHT A sizable audience to your content, whether through a bylined article in the opinion section of a popular publication, a book in the bestseller section of a bookstore, a keynote speaking slot at an exclusive conference, or all those and more, you have accomplished something special. Few aspiring thought leaders and their supporting casts *earn* those opportunities. And while they may not be on par with winning an Emmy, snaring an Oscar or entering the Baseball Hall of Fame, they are rare wins in the marketplace of people who try to get recognition for their expertise.

Yet I argue that in this digital world, you are better off *not* letting those noteworthy accomplishments directly produce inquiries. You are actually better off if a reader or conference attendee *doesn't* take the next step of calling or emailing you. The reason is that they are likely to be an undeveloped lead. They're an apple that looks appetizing on the tree but is not ripe enough to be picked.

You're much better off if they visit your website *first* to learn more about your firm. You want their last view of your firm's expertise to be on your firm's website.

Here's why: The thought leadership section of your website is the best place to shape your audience's understanding of you, your firm and what it can do for them. It can let you further educate prospective clients after they read or hear your first piece of content. You need the thought leadership part of your site to keep shaping their thinking to further attract those who like the way you think — *and* to deter those who don't.

You want your website's thought leadership section to be a great matchmaker between your firm, which has superior solutions to specific business problems, and organizations that have those problems.

In this chapter, I will explain why the thought leadership section of your website is the most important place to make much better matches between buyers (your audience) and sellers (your firm).

Think of it as the place where two people go to fall in love: Ideally, this happens once you've gotten to know each other well, not after the first glance or even the first date. The goal of your website should be to make sure that you and a potential client are 90 percent confident that, together as a pair, you are a great fit at solving their business problem. Your online content must let prospective clients explore what your firm can do and how you might work with them, so that they can become more convinced that the match would work.

Said another way, you want them to be largely sold that your firm is the best match for them before they talk to anyone in your organization. Doing that requires three changes:

- Shifting the center of gravity of thought leadership content to your website.

- Turning the site's thought leadership pages into a matchmaker between your firm and potential clients — one that enables both parties to get to know each other extremely well before they "date."

- Using data visualization tools surgically, not wantonly, to explain your firm's expertise clearly and compellingly and to allow viewers to "try it on."

Let's dive deep into how to design website pages that help turn viewers into ripe prospects.

PUTTING YOUR WEBSITE AT THE CENTER OF YOUR THOUGHT LEADERSHIP UNIVERSE

Most aspiring and actual thought leaders I know drive the people who like their ideas to the same place: their emails or phone numbers. Maybe it's because they want any business that stems from their ideas to come directly to them.

This is a vestige of the pre-web business world. That was a world I grew up in when I became a journalist in 1978, at a small Southern California newspaper. When you wanted to talk to someone as a source for an article, you needed their phone number. If they had a business card, you stapled that onto a blank card on your Rolodex. Or you called directory information and hoped the telephone operator had the listing.

By 1989, Lotus Notes was pioneering the use of email, with 35,000 subscribers; seven years later, Microsoft would introduce its earliest version of Outlook, which it called Internet Mail.[74] Email addresses became the way to reach out to someone you wanted to talk with, and those email addresses soon made their way onto your business card, right below your phone number. When companies started building their own websites (or outsourcing that to other firms) in the late 1990s, their website address made it on their business cards. But that website was the company's website, not a specific web page that featured their articles.

Nearly three decades later, many companies have yet to harness the thought leadership potential of their websites. Too many turn the web viewers' experience in learning about a firm's expertise into the equivalent of a drive through a city with no street signs. Occasionally a company might post an article by one of its consultants, with a short biography of the authors at the end — but not the authors' email addresses. If there is a click to contact, it might bring you to a page in which you insert your information. Even more important, if you want to learn more about the company's client work in the area that the author's article describes, that information is somewhere else in the site — if you can find it. You won't easily find client examples and testimonials that speak to the quality of the expertise that a firm has delivered.

In other words, the thought leadership sections of B2B websites are usually designed as dead ends — as educational content that sends interested viewers to a PDF. That's like getting on a train heading from Boston to New York City, having the track end at some small town in Connecticut that you never heard of, and being told the trip ends there. How do you get to your final destination? Nobody will tell you. That's your problem.

Here's the problem with most of the thought leadership website sections that I see, often tabbed **Insights**, **Knowledge**, **Expertise** or even **Thought Leadership**: They are one-directional communications about a better way to solve some problem. But they don't make it easy for readers who are intrigued enough to want to take the next step and find out much more about the experts behind that published expertise. Exactly who are the people whose bylines are atop the article? How did they gain their impressive knowledge? With what organizations have they done this work so that the reader can be more assured that they have done it well? How does the reader get in touch with these experts?

When the thought leadership content on your website does not help readers learn more about your experts and lead easily to one-on-one live conversations with them, you effectively have posted a dead-end sign — a remote station from which there's nowhere to go. Maybe they will keep digging into your firm's website to find more about the authors, their practice or their contact details.

But you've made it too hard for prospective clients. They have other viable options on their short list. That's a lost opportunity for you.

TURNING THE WEBSITE INTO A MATCHMAKING SITE

First, I must make a disclosure: I have never made a living by designing websites, not even the thought leadership section of websites. However, it doesn't stop me from having an opinion about how to optimally design the thought leadership sections of B2B websites. But to make sure my advice on this topic isn't simply from opinion, I will cite the observations and advice of others who are experts in this domain.

In the previous section, I made the point that the thought leadership content on a firm's website should not be the reader's final destination. With most digital media publications, after you've read the article, you're done or you're onto the next article. That's because the online media is not trying to sell you anything.

Of course, that's not the case with B2B firms that publish thought leadership on their websites. They *are* trying to sell their readers something. Consider, for a moment, that you could plot on a scale of 0 to 100 percent the degree to which a potential buyer is ready to say "yes," based on what he, she or a group of people are learning about their problem and a potentially better way to solve it (through your thought leadership content). Now imagine that this degree of "buy-in" happens over a period of time, based on how much more knowledge the prospective buyer gains about your experts and your firm.

Compelling thought leadership should help your firm move the buy-in needle from 0 percent to maybe 50 percent. That's far better than the typical cold call, when a salesperson out of the blue knocks on a customer's door and asks, "Do you have interest in our offerings?" At that point, there's zero buy-in. But it's not a cold call when clients have already discovered the thought leadership on your website, or your other thought leadership content outside that website (e.g., an op-ed in a popular magazine, a webinar, speech, etc.) that motivated them to visit your website and learn more. Those types of prospects are reaching out to *you,* rather than the other way around.

Yet even at this point, the most impressed reader may still be only about 50 percent bought into the firm's solution. You could gain another 10 to 30 percent buy-in if you revealed much more on your website. I see that content falling into five categories:

- **How your firm does the work:** Explaining how the project would be done — time, money, number of people required on both sides, etc.

- **Where your firm has done the work:** Case examples where you have delivered the services.

- **How successful the work has been:** Testimonials from those companies that speak to the quality and beneficial impact of the work.

- **Who does the work:** The backgrounds and client experiences of the people in your firm who do this work (in addition to your content authors).

- **How to start a conversation:** Contact information that (when provided) will get the ball rolling.

If you explained the above exceedingly well, you would have prospects who are 60 to 80 percent convinced that you're the right firm before they talk to anyone in your firm. Of course, these percentages are arbitrary and inexact. But you get the picture: These prospects are far more convinced that your firm is the go-to firm than they would have been had you only published your thought leadership content on your site — even if they had been captivated by one of your expert's conference speech or by her article in a prestigious journal.

A Website Built to Turn Thought Leadership Into Conversations

The number of smart B2B companies that have discovered the power of having a robust thought leadership section of their websites has increased over the past decade. Let's look at one of the best: Bain & Company's website. I base these observations solely on looking at the site, not from having any inside knowledge about it or how Bain operates (of which I have none).

Bain is a global management consulting firm. It publishes extensively on its website and in top-tier publications such as *Harvard Business Review*. But its website is where prospects can go much deeper on its content, practices, client work and the consultants who do that work.

I'll pick out just one of numerous Bain examples of how to present thought leadership and related content the right way: an article on mergers and acquisitions. Bain published the article — "Expanding M&A Options for New Capabilities" — on its website in February 2021. Here's what you can find easily in the article:

- **How Bain does the work:** Three links at the top and to the right of the article take you to three consulting services (corporate due diligence, divestitures and M&A). Each practice page provides a few paragraphs about the practice and its value to clients. They also have short videos from partners about the practice. Scroll down further and you'll see the number of projects that Bain has done.

- **Where Bain has done this work:** At the bottom of the article, the firm has a red box that explains three ways it has helped clients in M&A (divestiture, strategy and M&A).

Each case study is disguised (e.g., "HoldingCo, a large Latin American conglomerate"). Each case study web page follows the same structure: situation, approach, recommendations, results.

- **The impact of Bain's work for clients:** In each of the three case studies, Bain prominently provides the financial impact for clients (e.g., "12 percentage point increase in return on invested capital").

- **Who at Bain does the work:** The three authors are listed at the top of the article, and two of them have links to their bios. Each bio page has links to other content involving that person. One author has eight short video clips in which he talks about M&A. You can find more names of Bain M&A consultants at the bottom of the practice page — in fact, over 100 more. Clicking on a name or the picture leads to another bio page focused on that person.

- **Contact info:** At the bottom of the article is a contact form that doesn't mention the authors' names per se but asks if the reader is "Ready to talk?" Readers are asked to provide their email address so someone can contact them.

By making this information easy to find with a click from the article, Bain does a great job in giving you the salient information related to its M&A article. And that article is one of many on M&A on the Bain site. The firm makes it effortless for prospects to get a richer picture of Bain's M&A expertise and its impact.

USE DATA VISUALIZATION TO GENERATE EVEN MORE INTEREST IN YOUR EXPERTISE

The task of designing web pages that use incisive content to turn lukewarm prospects into fervent ones has been largely static for two decades. To be sure, short videos of authors discussing why they wrote their article have brought personality to the presentation.

But to strongly entice website visitors to explore what you can do, you need to harness the full capabilities of the online experience. The most forward-thinking news organizations and B2B companies are using infographics and data visualization in ways that leave their online visitors spellbound and engaged.

You might think infographics are a relatively "new-new" thing, discovered by B2B web content designers in the last decade. Colorful charts with images that bring survey data to life today are key elements of websites and social media campaigns. However, infographics have been used in media publications since at least 1982, when a national newspaper called *USA Today* began using flashy, catchy and colorful infographics on its front page to lure readers to those now-antiquated metal news boxes.

Newspapers and magazines have come a long way since then in putting such visuals to use. The dynamic websites of such publications as *The New York Times*, *Washington Post* and *National Geographic* have been redefining what digital graphics can do to help journalists and photographers explain the issues they report on. Data visualization, digital video, podcasts and other digital media formats have been bringing their stories to life. Perhaps it's been a key factor behind why digital subscriptions at these media companies have exploded over the last decade, while their print readership shrank. By May 2021, *The New York Times'* 7.8 million subscribers included 6.9 million who were digital only.[75] At media properties that do it well, the digital news experience — a reader's learning about a timely issue through reporting — is far superior to the print news experience.

These are welcome developments to the game of thought leadership: i.e., educating people in organizations with problems looking for experts who can solve them. Many of these techniques and technologies need to be embraced by B2B designers of the thought leadership experience. Thought leadership professionals should pay more attention than media companies do to certain visual techniques — call them argument enhancers — than to others. The reason is that the goal of journalism is very different than the goal of thought leadership:

- **The goal of journalism:** To shed light on important issues and news events. The focus here is on bringing truth and understanding about the existence of an issue or problem.

- **The goal of thought leadership:** To shed light on better ways of solving significant organizational, individual and societal problems. The focus of thought leadership content is on how to *solve* the problem, showing examples of organizations, people, countries, etc. that have solved it for the better. Journalists don't have that obligation. Their crucial role in society is to shine light on issues.

For thought leadership professionals, this requires substantially rethinking the design of content pages. Most of all, it means shifting from a print mindset to a digital mindset.

That is easier said than done. Working with printed publications for so long has shackled the way many designers and editors put content online. The print paradigm leads to the following short-sighted approaches to explaining complex topics:

- Favoring prose over images, or confining images such as charts, graphs, photos, etc., to lower-class status.

- Seeing content as one-way communication, a digital sermon of sorts — saying, in effect, "Here's my argument, laid out in 5,000 words. Hope you like it."

In contrast, designing thought leadership content for the web viewer requires a broader palette of illustrative devices. The static "ink" of words, pictures, graphs, photos and illustrations needs to be supplemented with the dancing pixels of video, interactive charts, digital voices and other images that move, make sound and allow you to see people and places.

What's more, the communication needs to be more than one-directional. The viewer should be able to customize a chart to her specific interests — e.g., tools that filter the information to show how some problem is playing out in India, not just Indiana. The ultimate interactivity of the thought leadership content on a website is allowing the viewer to "try on" your diagnosis of his company's problems. This can — and is — being done today with benchmarking surveys that allow viewers to compare how they're handling some problem vs. how a set of best-practice companies that took a survey are handling it.

But like many things "digital," the costs for videos, interactive charts, podcasts, etc. can add up. These bells and whistles can also become quite seductive to marketers, web designers and thought leadership content developers — and the thought leaders themselves. What aspiring thought leader would not want a professionally produced video of her discussing why she authored an article on her favorite issue? What better way to gain personal visibility — externally and internally?

This is where I need to urge some caution. At some point, the value of digital videos, podcasts, interactive charts and other elaborate digital ways to enhance thought leadership content will diminish. Passing the point of diminishing returns means you will be throwing additional resources toward making an argument that is already soundly presented.

The question is this: With so many ways to convey an argument online today beyond prose, and with each way meaning extra cost, which ones do you use? And not use? And why? And how do you know when you have reached that point of diminishing returns?

DIGITALLY PRESENTING THOUGHT LEADERSHIP CONTENT: DISCERNING WHAT WILL WORK BEST

Once again, I need to start with a caveat: I am *not* a data visualization expert. Or a website expert. Or a video, audio, photo or any other type of expert on these media. I am *not* going to tell you how to build stunning infographics or interactive graphics, take memorable photos or record compelling videos or audio content.

Nonetheless, I *do* have strong opinions about what types of imagery — interactive or static (essentially meaning you can't click to change it) — would better convey arguments about superior ways to solve complex problems. I say this because I believe the first-order knowledge here is largely *not* about how to do videos and audio content, or how to design and build interactive charts. Rather, it's about how such imagery can help viewers comprehend a complex argument.

With that admittedly long-winded warning, I believe one good way (but certainly not the only) to think about this issue is to start with the six pieces of a thought leader's argument that I laid out in Chapter 6: problem, why existing solutions fall short, new solution in brief, new solution in detail, how to overcome the key challenges to adopting the new solution and why firms should move now. The issue of how to use *online* visualization comes down to this: How would it help thought leaders increase their audience's ability to believe in their argument?

I see seven ways in which online technology — including websites, data visualization software (e.g., Tableau), digital video and audio, and other tools we have in the tool chest — can help thought leaders get bigger buy-in to their arguments:

- **Illustrative imagery:** These are literal or figurative images (photos, illustrations) that help describe a topic and its seriousness. An excellent example is the "glass ceiling" concept, which illustrates the invisible barriers that women face in moving up in organizations. We all know that we can't go higher than a room's ceiling, but we think we might if it's glass and thus hard to see, until we realize that we can't break the glass. Perfect words — howsoever depicted through imagery — to connote this concept.

- **Trend depiction:** Trend depiction is done through charts and graphs that show how some phenomenon has changed over time (revenue, costs, quality problems, customer turnover, etc.), or how it compares across regions, age groups and other categories. It also can be done through a series of photographs of the same phenomenon taken over time (e.g., the evolution of the skyline of a city over decades, or of a neighborhood and its storefronts).

- **Emotional pleas:** These are graphics/audio (photos, videos) of people who directly or indirectly help viewers make a visceral connection to a problem in the world, or a better way to solve it. Since the beginning of photography, this visual and auditory imagery has made people experience the horrors of war, demonstrations and other historic moments. Memorable photos/videos depict wars (e.g., the 1972 photo by Huynh Thanh My, of people running away from burning buildings), demonstrations (the famous 1970 John Filo photo at Kent State showing the horror of a young woman standing over one of the four students who was killed) and other famous incidents (e.g., George Floyd's horrible death at the knee of a Minneapolis police officer). The audio of the 1937 Hindenburg crash in New Jersey brings back the horror of that tragic day. Although the imagery to make their emotional pleas are less likely to show such violence, thought leadership content presenters can also draw on photos, videos and audio to get their points across.

- **First-hand confirmation:** This would be videos and audio from people who can vouch for a significant organizational problem and its solution.

- **Unifying frameworks:** Thought leadership, at its best, simplifies complex issues. Nothing is better than a graphic framework to draw out the key elements of the solution and show how they relate to one another. Seeing a graphic of this — boxes connected to other boxes, for example — can make the solution far easier to comprehend than if you used prose alone.

- **Visual comparisons:** Comparing conventional solutions to a superior solution is important if thought leaders want to demonstrate that their answer to a problem is better. In a static world, using tables whose columns compare average-practice benefits with best-practice benefits makes the comparisons easier to see. The online interactive world can make for much better visual comparisons.

- **Experiential simulation:** Online, you can pretend you're flying a plane, taking a roller-coaster ride or walking through a house. If you work at an architecture firm and design better dorms, why not take the viewer through a walk-through that shows what it's like to move through those dorms? If you work at a management consulting firm that optimizes manufacturers' supply chains, why not create a computer image that lets viewers see how their own network of plants and warehouses would have to change if they cut their number of plants by 50 percent and expanded the remaining ones? How would that impact the number of warehouses, and the transportation volume to them?

While those techniques could be used to amplify any of the six elements of a thought leader's argument, some are more useful than others in explaining certain elements. The table that follows lays out how they could be used in each argument piece (plus one for the upfront summary).

0. INTRODUCTION AND SUMMARY

What the content is about, why the authors believe it's important, and why it's worth the veiwers' time
Illustrative Imagery: Set overall visual (type of problem) and tone (on its seriousness)
Emotional Pleas: Video of authors and/or people and orgs suffering from problem

1. PROBLEM ESTABLISHMENT

The proof that indeed, there is a big and widespread problem
Trend depiction: Charts and graphs showing evolution and severity of problem

2. EXISTING SOLUTION SHORTCOMINGS

That mainstream solutions are hugely inadequate
Trend depiction: Charts and graphs showing low impact of existing solutions

3. NEW, SUPERIOR SOLUTION, BENEFITS AND PROOF (EXAMPLES IN BRIEF)

That the authors' new solutions is very different - and very effective
First-hand confirmation: Table showing beneficiaries (companies that adopted the soluion) and benefits they achieved
Unifying framework: Conceptual graphics showing relationship among core soliution elements
Visual Comparison: Charts, tables or other graphics comparing impact of new solution to existing solutions

4. NEW SOLUTION PROCESS AND ILLUSTRATIVE CASE EXAMPLES

That the new solution is well -thought-out and adoptable/practical
First-hand confirmation: Pictures and videos of orgs that have used the solutions; charts on benefits
Unifying framework: Conceptual graphic on individual elements of solution
Visual Comparison: Charts or tables showing "before" and "after" metrics (revenue, cost, quality, time to market, etc.)

5. KEY ADOPTION OBSTACLES AND AROUND THEM

That the authors are well-versed in the org adoption obstacles, can help you overcome them
Illustrative Imagery: Icons or other images signifying key adoption barriers
First Hand Communication: Videos of people from orgs (and/or authors) to explain how barriers to adoption were overcome

6. CASE FOR MOVING NOW AND NEXT STEPS

How to start on the right path to solving the problem in the new way
Trend Depiction: Interactive charts that let viewers see potential impact of not trying to solve problem, based on projections of key trends
Emotional Pleas: Video of authors and/or people from orgs that solved the problem, explaining importance of solving
Experiential Simulation: Interactive surveys for viewers to see magnitude of potential benefits they could achieve

Content/POV Structure/Outline	Illustrative Imagery	Trend Depiction	Emotional Pleas
0. Introduction and summary	Set overall visual (type of problem) and tone (on its seriousness)		Video of authors and/or people and orgs suffering from problem
1. Problem establishment		Charts and graphs showing evolution and severity of problem	
2. Existing solution shortcomings		Charts and graphs showing low impact of existing solutions	
3. New, superior solution, benefits and proof (examples in brief)			
4. New solution process and illustrative case examples			
5. Key adoption obstacles and path around them	Icons or other images signifying key adoption barriers		
6. Case for moving now and first steps		Interactive charts that let viewers see potential impact of not trying to solve problem, based on projections of key trends	Video of authors and/or people from orgs that solved the problem, explaining importance of solving

ARGUMENT VISUAL ENHANCERS			
First-Hand Confirmation	Unifying Framework	Visual Comparison	Experiential Simulation
Table showing beneficiaries (companies that adopted the soluion) and benefits they achieved	Conceptual graphics showing relationship among core soliution elements	Charts, tables or other graphics comparing impact of new solution to existing solutions	
Pictures and videos of orgs that have used the solutions; charts on benefits	Conceptual graphic on individual elements of solution	Charts or tables showing "before" and "after" metrics (revenue, cost, quality, time to market, etc.)	
Videos of people from orgs (and/or authors) to explain how barriers to adoption were overcome			
			Interactive surveys for viewers to see magnitude of potential benefits they could achieve

Now let's look at these techniques through the lens of the outline structure. To illustrate them, I'll draw on compelling examples from the media and non-media-company world.

Introduction & Summary: Setting an Overall Tone

For a print publication, this page would be the cover, and for an online publication the first screen. For both print and online, the goal is to give the viewer a powerful first look — a striking image and a memorable headline that captures the essence of the argument and makes it an irresistible read.

From a visualization standpoint, this is where illustrative imagery plays a big role. I'm not talking about hackneyed "art" — the photo with models around a conference table, dressed sharply in business attire and faking an animated discussion. We're all used to, and maybe repelled by, such stock art. While it does save readers from having to dive into a wall of dense prose, the images subtly signal that this will be one more predictable and forgettable article.

This should not, of course, be what such opening images portray if you want viewers to keep reading. What you want is compelling yet illustrative imagery. I say "illustrative" because you don't want a compelling image that has little if anything to do with the content's topic. Commissioning an accomplished artist to do an illustration, cartoon or painting that is visually striking yet still abstract is a waste of talent and money. It's gratuitous art, meant perhaps to liven up what you might think is a deadly dull topic, or a deadly treatment of it. That is *not* how thought leadership content should be portrayed.

Instead, your image has to illustrate that core concept — your point of view on a specific problem or your unique solution to it. Some of the best illustrative imagery I've seen in thought leadership is on the covers of *Harvard Business Review's* print magazine. One of its best covers in recent years (for *HBR's* September-October 2020 edition) memorably and quickly explained a problem with many HR management strategies: They take a formulaic, one-size-fits-all approach to managing employees. The cover featured a metallic cookie cutter in the shape of a person. The image, with the article title inside it ("Where People Management Went Wrong"), instantly conveys the problem. Great visual.

How could a digital version of that image convey the message even better? Here's one idea: an animation of a long line of people shaped as cookies — different sizes, colors, genders, etc. — entering a door on the left side of a building. As they exit the building from a door on the right, you see they've been "re-stamped" with the same mold.

Problem Establishment

Once you've gained your audience's attention through striking illustrative imagery, you have to prove the problem you are writing about is a real one. Trend depictions can be helpful here in getting viewers to see the severity of a problem.

One of the best ways thought leaders can raise the alarm about a problem is by showing how it stacks up to similar problems. A great example of this is a graphic from a data visualization expert and colleague of mine, Bill Shander. In the early months of the COVID-19 pandemic, many people (including the U.S. White House) were minimizing how bad things could get. The COVID death rate would be no worse than the flu death rate, according to one line of thinking. By July 2020, deaths in the U.S. were nearing 150,000. That prompted Shander to depict on his website (billshander.com) just how lethal the virus had become, compared with other leading killers of Americans. As Shander showed, the virus had overtaken strokes as the fifth-leading cause of deaths at that point, far surpassing the flu (the eighth-leading cause). By the time 2020 ended, the U.S. Centers for Disease Control and Prevention proclaimed COVID-19 to be America's third-leading cause of death that year, trailing only cancer and heart disease. In the first two months of 2021, COVID-19 moved into the No. 1 place.

COVID-19 WILL BE (AT LEAST) THE #3 KILLER IN THE US IN 2020

Leading causes of death data (2017) from CDC https://www.cdc.gov/ncha/fastats/leading-causes-of-death.htm)
COVID-19 cumulative deaths data from Our World in Data (https://ourworldindata.org/coronavirus-source-data)

Credit: Bill Shander

Another great example of helping viewers intimately understand the seriousness of a problem comes from *The New York Times'* digital edition. One of the *Times'* reporters wrote a story in 2021 about rising sea levels. A vividly colored scrolling graphic depicted how climate change would affect every country in the world, and let viewers interact with it to get a more detailed look at how it will affect where they live.

Graphically depicted emotional pleas can provide the most striking evidence of the cost of a problem. Seeing its impact on individuals is a tactic used for decades in politics, to draw attention to otherwise abstract policies and complex debates about the need for laws that change the status quo.

Nothing strikes the heartstrings of a problem better than hearing from people who are suffering from it. The online world allows us to go beyond running photos. McKinsey's website has done a remarkable job of this during the pandemic, including in one interactive part of its COVID Response Center on McKinsey.com. The web page (called "The Emotion Archive") announces itself as an interactive site where viewers can see, hear and read how 122 people in eight countries had been affected by the pandemic in April and May 2020 — from the people themselves.

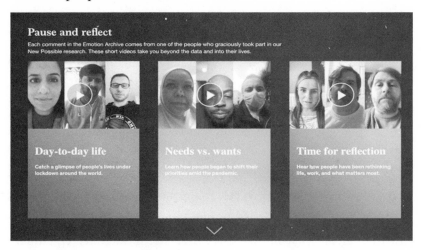

Credit: McKinsey & Company Webpage

The consulting firm then categorizes 800 comments it heard from these people into buckets like "joy," "trust," "surprise" and "sadness." Depicted as circles of different sizes (determined by how many comments fell in that category), you can see how "acceptance" and "apprehension" are the two most common emotions. Then scroll down more and you can see short videos of people from their homes talking about their lives, priorities and perspectives on life, work and "what matters most." If McKinsey, via its thought leadership, is trying to show it knows the pandemic has taken a big toll on humanity, this page communicates it well. The people who were polled and video-taped provide the emotion.

Why Existing Solutions Fall Short

Thought leaders need to compare their solutions to those that are already in play. A thought leader doesn't become a thought leader until he or she is recognized for a unique and superior solution to some problem in the world. It is here where visual comparisons can work wonders.

The New York Times site excels at this. A recent example is an article it published in February 2021 about how public schools could reduce the spread of the coronavirus in their classrooms.[76] By scrolling down, viewers could see a three-dimensional illustration of a classroom that morphs and evolves. The first depicts a pre-COVID view with 28 students and one teacher, with the windows closed. As viewers scroll, they see a second scene depicting the early days of COVID, with nine masked students spaced apart and one teacher, also with windows closed. Vectors show how, despite wearing masks, students are breathing in recirculated air from one another. The third visual shows windows still closed (with one infected student in the room) and how the air flow is spreading the infected student's COVID germs throughout the room. The last scenarios show an open window and how the outside air dilutes the air's contaminants and reduces their spread, and another scenario with an air cleaner and box fan bringing fresh outside air into the room, which dilutes the contaminants even more.

New Solutions

No imagery is as important to thought leadership as the graphic treatment of a unifying framework. "Perspective is worth 50 IQ points," Alan Kay once remarked. He was one of the technology whizzes at Xerox's famed Palo Alto, CA, research laboratory in the 1970s, whose inventions helped birth the first Apple Macintosh. (Xerox PARC, for Palo Alto Research Center, was what the lab was called.) Kay knows the power of thought leadership, even if he doesn't use those two words.

Having a powerful framework in thought leadership is worth another 50 IQ points. Memorable ones that made their inventors famous include Harvard Business School Professor Michael Porter's value chain and five forces frameworks. Boston Consulting Group became famous in the 1960s with its growth-share matrix (with its "stars," "cash cows," "dogs" and "question marks").

Are there digital versions of compelling frameworks today that help viewers better grasp the concepts that they illustrate? I haven't found any. But perhaps there's a big opportunity here. If there is, such interactive frameworks would have to provide more value than their static, one-dimensional antecedents in ways such as these:

- **Showing what happens when one element gets out of whack.** Take the reengineering diamond framework. What would happen if a company's values and beliefs changed dramatically? How might that affect the performance of people working in a streamlined, cross-functional business process?

- **Showing what happens when certain elements of a framework are fully digitized.** Take Porter's value chain — the sequence of steps that a manufacturer takes to turn raw materials into products that it sells in the marketplace (inbound logistics > manufacturing > distribution > marketing > selling). Newspapers, magazines, records, video games and other media used to be physical products. (To some extent, they still are.) But for those that have become purely digital products, how might that change the age-old value chain framework? If you nuke the manufacturing and physical distribution of a product, does that put pressure to dramatically improve the other key elements? Does it substantially raise the importance of creating awareness (i.e., marketing) of the now-online product, given that owning printing presses, vinyl-making plants, DVD-making plants, etc. — and having retail distribution (newsstands, news boxes, record stores, video game retailers, etc.) — no longer matters? Of course, it does. What if there were a new value chain, made interactive on a website, that would let a viewer plug in such things as "My product is becoming digital" to see which parts of the value chain become more important, and why?

Overcoming the Adoption Barriers to Existing Solutions

If readers start to believe in a new, superior solution but wonder whether their organization can implement it, how can thought leaders get them to see that those barriers are surmountable? One of the best ways is to let those readers hear directly from organizations that overcame the barriers — i.e., through case study videos.

It's one thing for the thought leaders' firm to present how its clients overcame the adoption barriers. It's a whole other thing to hear directly from those clients themselves. A testimonial is much more credible than a consulting firm tooting its own horn. And another way is to get them to envision the future solution — in essence, to "try it on" digitally through experiential simulation.

The Case for Moving Now, and First Steps

This final part of an interactive piece of thought leadership content can be the most effective one in moving tire-kickers to highly interested buyers. If viewers are captivated by everything they have read on your website, this could be an excellent time to have them take an interactive online survey — right from your site — that asks them a number of questions gauging the severity of the problem in their company.

If you have conducted a survey of several hundred or thousands of companies on your topic and you've compared best and work practices among the survey participants, you could also make this interactive tool a device by which potential clients compare what they've done with best-practice firms. In essence, this will be a crude benchmarking tool.

And if you offer to provide additional insights via a phone call on how they compare vs. the best-practice firms, that could become a very productive session for your firm's sales force.

Using data visualization and other tools to enhance how websites educate prospects on better ways to solve their problems is a new frontier in thought leadership. Companies that compete on thought leadership have recognized this. They've staffed up with experts in these areas and are looking closely at how the best media companies do it.

PART V

SCALING EXPERTISE

CHAPTER 9

CONVERTING THOUGHT LEADERSHIP INTO HIGH-QUALITY SERVICES

+   +   +   +   +   +   +   +

THE TWO PREVIOUS CHAPTERS examined the thought leadership marketing by which many of the best firms I know attract clients. Increasingly, as I explained in Chapter 8, companies whose websites make a powerful case about their unique expertise turn lukewarm tire-kickers into serious prospects.

This is *demand creation* at its best.

However, firms that excel only at demand creation have accomplished just half of what is necessary to compete on thought leadership. The other half is *supply creation*. Unfortunately, from my experience, thought leadership supply creation has been largely ignored. Far more attention has been cast on content development and demand creation.

That's an unsustainable practice. A consulting, law, architecture or other B2B firm's superior answer to a complex business problem is only a superior answer on paper. It doesn't become a superior *solution* to clients' problems until a firm can deliver its solution at scale and with high quality. That, in turn, requires a firm to master three pieces of *supply creation*:

- **Methodology development:** Taking frameworks and knowledge from best practices and incorporating them into project approaches, tools and training modules by which others in their firm can learn how to do the work.

- **Recruiting, and training & development:** Hiring people with the requisite competencies to do the work, and training them on the new methodologies and tools.

- **Delivery:** Organizing these people into teams so they learn about one another and how to collaborate on projects.

In my career, I haven't seen B2B companies focus nearly as much on the supply creation side of thought leadership as on the demand creation side. As I argued earlier, I see it as the fundamental factor that brought down CSC Index. Developing and bringing a blockbuster idea to market is exhilarating. But if the firm that created that idea can't implement it consistently well with many clients, the goodwill it earned by being the pioneer will vanish.

Word of lackluster projects, and project failures, soon will get around to other firms. The allure of working with the pioneer will fade quickly. Having seen the pioneer create a robust market for a new class of expertise, competitors will swoop in. They'll essentially say, "We do that too, and we do it better."

Competitors that are better at the *supply creation* end of thought leadership will run away with the market. They will have scaled up the delivery of their expertise — that is, the number of employees who have been trained well to bring a new and better solution to dozens and perhaps even hundreds of clients. This applies to any professional services or other B2B firm that decides to compete on thought leadership — law, accounting, investment banking, architecture, IT services, training and development, and others. They must deliver their expertise at mass scale.

The failure to do this well enough is what left CSC Index behind after it created the market for reengineering consulting services in 1990. By 1995, that market was estimated by Gartner as a $4.7 billion-a-year global business. That meant that in 1995, Index (with $200 million in revenue) had only 4 percent of the market. Three other firms had become much bigger players: Andersen Consulting ($700 million in reengineering consulting revenue), McKinsey ($540 million) and Ernst & Young ($520 million).[77] In fact, by 2000, CSC Index, the pioneer of business reengineering consulting, had shut its doors altogether.

If you come up with a blockbuster approach to solving a complex business problem and market and sell it effectively, but you can't solve the problem at scale, you will have created a big market for your competition — a market that you will later abdicate.

In short, if a company's demand creation activities make promises about having superior expertise, it must be able to honor those promises. Otherwise, someone else will.

Let's explore why, as I see it, the supply side of thought leadership has received so little attention.

WHY SUPPLY CREATION IS USUALLY AN ORPHAN

I see three main reasons why the supply side of thought leadership is typically ignored or given scant attention: lack of incentives for the content developers; a skills and interests mismatch between them and the people charged with scaling up expertise; and firm leaders' delusion that the expense is unnecessary (especially when demand for their firm's expertise is exploding).

If you leave it up to your thought leaders to scale up your firm's expertise, you may wait a long time. The spoils of being recognized as a thought leader — keynote speeches at prestigious conferences, opinion column writing opportunities, private presentations to leaders of big organizations that could become clients — are time-consuming. I've seen this play out several times in my career: thought leaders who (once they became recognized) grew more interested in giving highly paid speeches and armchair consulting assignments than they were in helping ramp up their firm's capabilities.

Liz Wiseman has seen this too. Her firm, the Wiseman Group, develops management training aimed at "ridding the world of bad bosses," as she puts it. She wrote a 2010 *New York Times* bestseller (*Multipliers: How the Best Leaders Make Everyone Smart*), and she focuses on turning her research-based ideas into methodologies that training companies like Franklin Covey and BTS convert into training products. She calls herself "a learning designer at heart."

Wiseman said too many thought leaders seem to be focused on "the most lucrative parts of this work: to drop into a firm as 'edutainment,' collect their fees and go home." For example, Wiseman once asked a well-known thought leader how he helps companies implement his ideas. "His answer was, 'I don't care about that,'" she said, adding, "He's just making money from speaking."[78]

As Wiseman told me, "It's easier to turn thought leadership into valuable services if you're there to serve the client." What an apt way to put it!

Any debate about whether your firm's newly made thought leaders should spend more time in the marketplace generating interest, or more time inside the firm getting others to deliver some new expertise, is likely to be a short one. Revenue speaks loudest. Your rainmakers won't want to be constrained from making rain — especially if your company's reward system focuses more on individual performance and less on firm performance.

Even if the incentives encourage your thought leaders to share their knowledge internally, their personalities and thinking styles may get in the way. "The skills for becoming a thought leader and the skills for methodology development are very different," Shane Cragun, a senior partner at leadership development and recruiting giant Korn Ferry, explained to me.[79] Cragun knows of what he speaks. For seven years, he headed delivery of training for Franklin Covey Co., the firm that capitalized on Stephen R. Covey's blockbuster 1989 book, *The 7 Habits of Highly Effective People.*

Cragun uses the classic Whole Brain Model of Ned Herrmann to compare how thought leaders think against how people who excel at methodology development (also known as instructional designers) and training think.[80] The thought leaders tend to be in the upper-right quadrant of the model — off the scale in being theoretical and intuitive (holistic, experimental, integrating and synthesizing). In contrast, methodology professionals' thinking styles are in the lower-left sphere: rational and realistic (organized, sequential, planned and detailed).

Trainers, on the other hand, tend to be lower right, Cragun believes. "The skills for the thought leaders and the skills for methodology developers are almost diametrically opposed," he said.

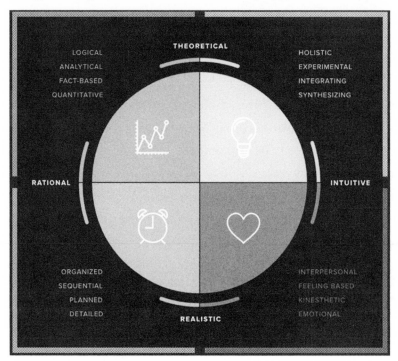

Copyright and Courtesy of Herrmann Global, LLC

Dave Ulrich, a recognized thought leader since the 1990s on leadership, organizational change and human resource management issues, has a similar view. He points to the difficult trade-offs between discovery and delivery mentioned in his writings on innovation. "Discovery is about creativity, fresh thinking, new ideas," Ulrich said. In contrast, "delivery is about turning ideas into impact."[81] If professional services firms don't turn their intellectual property into standardized frameworks and processes, they have a hard time growing, he added.

I believe the third reason why many companies ignore or skimp on the supply side of thought leadership is the biggest: With leads coming in from everywhere, top management sees no reason to ramp up the skill level of their workforce. Demand is off the charts. Taking consultants, lawyers, architects or other professionals offline for training and education would come with a severe hit to revenue, billable hours and profitability. (That's in part what kept CSC Index's leaders from investing heavily in internal methodology and training of the firm's consultants, one former management team member told me.[82]) In addition, leaders could assume their smart people will "figure it out" on the job — i.e., on the client's nickel. If they don't, some leaders might wonder whether clients will know the difference.

You don't want your firm to ignore the supply side of thought leadership. There is a better way.

CONDUCTING DEMAND- AND SUPPLY-CREATION CONCURRENTLY

Companies that scale up their expertise while they're scaling up their marketing and sales resources are those that take delivery seriously. They also think about delivery while thought leadership research is ongoing. Three moves are important:

Align Thought Leaders' Incentives With the Company's Incentives

If your thought leaders are rewarded only on marketing and sales metrics — revenue, leads generated, conference presentations delivered, website downloads, etc. — you will be motivating them to continue doing things that generate more revenue and leads. They'll look for more speaking opportunities, more writing opportunities, more chances to get in front of prospects who are ready to buy.

But they won't be motivated to do much else — especially, to deliver excellent project work, train your people on how to do the work and ensure clients are happy with the work. That will only happen if your thought leaders are also measured on such supply-side metrics as client satisfaction and client impact.

Assign Methodology and Training Pros as Part-Time Members of the R&D Team

To shorten the time it takes for methodology development professionals to convert thought leadership concepts into training modules, companies should make one of the method-makers a part-time member of the research team. In this way, your methodology people can begin scoping out the training modules. And by moving some of your internal trainers through the research team, they can begin to hear the best-practice stories that your researchers are collecting. Those trainers then will be able to tell those stories with much greater authority in internal training exercises because they heard them first-hand.

Researchers, methodology developers and trainers need to understand their roles here:

- **Researchers:** Spot trends, analyze what the firms that are best at solving the problem are doing differently, come up with frameworks that diagnose and solve the problem.

- **Methodology developers:** Take emerging thinking on best practices and turn them into rigorous methods that can be taught internally. They are there to absorb the research and not to hem in the researchers on what they are seeing.

- **Trainers:** Determine how to best teach the methods and the case stories that prove they work.

Cragun of Korn Ferry said: "The perfect team is the thought leader, the instructional designer and the workshop teacher. The teacher is the one who is clarifying the principles. The thought leader has sway over what this and that means. The learning designer must think about, 'How do we actually teach that? What are the steps?' And the teacher/delivery person is the person saying, 'That's not going to work in the classroom. We need to put a heartfelt story in at that point.'"

SEEDING CONTENT DEVELOPMENT WITH CAPABILITY DEVELOPMENT

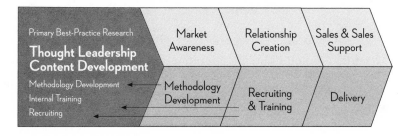

Your thought leadership researchers, methodology developers and trainers might not be comfortable working together at first. But as long as they understand what they're there to do, and they recognize their thinking preferences, that should go a long way to integrating the thought leadership R&D team. Perhaps most of all, they need to respect their roles and contributions to supply creation. Any "intellectual superiority" of team members — i.e., thought leaders and researchers looking down on the rest — must go away.

Ulrich wrote about how this pecking order works in academia. In a recent paper, he said that many college professors "believe in a hierarchy of knowledge providers, with those who explore theory/research and publish in 'A' journals followed by those who teach next-generation students, followed by consultants who offer advice, and ultimately managers who take action." Ulrich said those comparisons lead to disrespect from each perspective. "Academics might label practitioners as quick-fix charlatans, purveyors of silver bullets, or faddish. Practitioners might label academics as ivory tower, eggheads, abstract and quixotic."[83]

You don't want that kind of caste structure in your thought leadership R&D and supply creation teams.

Track the Delivery of Your Services as Rigorously as you Track the Revenue Stream

Your marketing and sales groups should be tracking the lead stream from thought leadership demand creation. But the tracking shouldn't end there. The goal of the supply creation side is for the company to have substantial beneficial impact on clients' business. To do that, people should be assigned to auditing the progress of projects in the works, and the projects that have been completed. Where are they getting bogged down? Why? What methods need tweaking, or more? What skills do project teams need more of, or less of?

To compete on thought leadership over the long haul, and not be a shooting star like CSC Index and many other once-prominent thought leaders, companies must put as much rigor and effort into supply creation as they put into demand creation.

The pioneers of a blockbuster concept must master the supply creation part of thought leadership — if they want to be continually regarded as the superior solution.

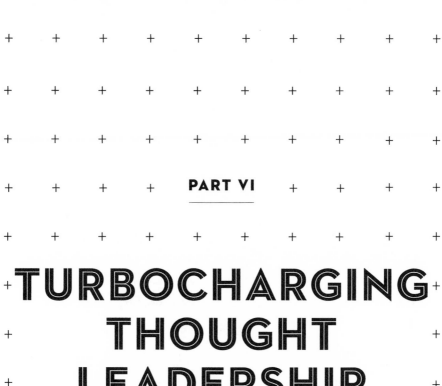

PART VI

TURBOCHARGING THOUGHT LEADERSHIP

CHAPTER 10

TURNING COMPANY LEADERS INTO DEVOUT ADVOCATES

+   +   +   +   +   +   +   +

T HE PREVIOUS NINE CHAPTERS explained how to compete on the core elements of thought leadership. We've deeply explored how a number of B2B organizations became regarded as the superior solution to their clients' problems, even if just for a short period. We saw how their thought leadership activities helped them grow faster and more profitably than their competitors.

Yet for every company I know that is fully bought into thought leadership and couldn't imagine operating as anything but a thought leader, I know of 10 others whose leaders remain skeptical about it. Most of them invest in it but don't have high hopes that the return will be sizable, or even measurable. They look at it as a necessary expense — just like having an attractive employee benefits package.

Thought leadership can only become a competitive advantage in organizations whose leaders are devoted to it. While they may be initially skeptical, they must grow into devout advocates.

The *Cambridge Dictionary* defines devout as "believing strongly in a religion and obeying all its rules or principles." Thought leadership, of course, is not a religion. However, to compete on the basis of creating, delivering and marketing superior expertise, leaders must deeply believe that thought leadership is how their organization will compete in the marketplace.

It's easy for company leaders to fall quickly in and out of love with thought leadership. This is especially true during economic downturns, when chief marketing officers who became giddy about thought leadership watch in disbelief after the rug is pulled out from under them. Without strong pull from the top — a deep understanding by the people who run the firm about what thought leadership is and how it can propel the firm — adequate thought leadership investments are not likely to be sustained.

In my experience, few B2B chief executives other than those running professional services and research firms — companies whose clients pay them for their expertise — view thought leadership as vital to success. And even leaders of companies that invest heavily in thought leadership can wonder whether they're spending too much. That thinking happens when leaders haven't seen it move the needle on leads, revenue and profits.

I've written this book for a wide spectrum of audiences: companies that at some point will have to compete on thought leadership but don't know it yet (call them "the extreme skeptics"); companies that would like to believe that thought leadership could grow their businesses, have been trying to do it but haven't seen the returns yet (call them "hopeful skeptics"); and companies that already compete on the basis of thought leadership (the "advocates") and thus don't need convincing. If anything, they want to raise their game.

I've written this chapter for all three of those audiences, but especially for the hopeful skeptics. Their leaders want to believe in the power of thought leadership. But they lack tangible proof that it is worthy of substantial investment — not only in money but also the time their internal subject experts must spend to get recognized in the marketplace for their expertise.

TURNING THE HOPEFUL SKEPTICS INTO ADHERENTS

Admittedly, I know that competing on thought leadership in the ways I have laid out in this book will be too much for some B2B firms to embrace. It will be a tall order for the "hopeful but skeptical" crowd to accept. They have dipped their toes into thought leadership. Perhaps some of their thought leaders and marketing leaders have urged senior management to increase the budget. But when the budget holders are skeptical about the value of thought leadership, those budget discussions are likely to remain debates, and often tense ones.

Over the last two decades, this has been a constant frustration for me, given my experience of helping ignite the multibillion-dollar market for business reengineering services in the 1990s. I chalk it up to the fact that the practice of thought leadership is still nascent at B2B companies (though it's farther along in the professional services segment). Compared with the state of R&D in the software or pharmaceutical industries, or the state of marketing in the consumer products sector, the practice of thought leadership is in a far less advanced stage.

For sure, the practice of thought leadership is not in a primordial state any longer. But from my experience and research, even the best companies at thought leadership are only best at certain aspects of it. Some are exceptional at content development but not audience-building. Others are strong marketers but inconsistent at producing exceptional content. And even companies that are highly skilled at developing and marketing content typically fall down on the delivery-of-services side. In other words, no B2B firm I know of has snapped together all the pieces of the thought leadership puzzle.

Maybe that's because the thought leadership profession — if you can call it a profession — is far less understood than, say, the R&D profession in software and pharma, or the marketing profession in consumer products. In those industries, academic, government and other research has focused on R&D and marketing practices for decades. But that's not the case for B2B thought leadership, even in the professional services slice of B2B, where the very thing these firms sell is expertise.

The studies I have led on the thought leadership profession — six in all — since 2005 are among the few that have been conducted. Nonetheless, two that we did with Rattleback in the last three years indicate that competence at thought leadership comes with practice over time, and that firms with greater impact also have stronger advocates at the top.

SHORTENING THE BUY-IN CURVE

Our surveys in 2018 and 2020 of more than 300 thought leadership professionals each year found that B2B firms with longer experience in creating, marketing and selling superior content were likely to be better at this game than firms with less experience. The most successful of the 300+ survey participants in 2020 ("most successful" defined as being extremely effective at generating market awareness and leads) worked in firms that had been doing thought leadership an average 70 percent longer than the firms with the least effective thought leadership activities — 7.6 years vs. 4.4 years.

LONGEVITY'S IMPACT ON THOUGHT LEADERSHIP MARKETING SUCCESS
(# of Years that Leaders and Followers Have been Doing TL Marketing, by % of Respondents)

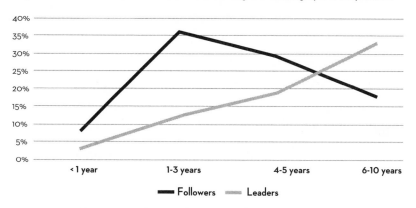

At the same time, the most successful firms at thought leadership were three times more likely to have company leaders who viewed thought leadership to be extremely important to revenue growth. Some 64 percent of these "leaders" said top management in their firms view thought leadership as vital to increasing revenue. Another 29 percent said it was "very important" to sales growth. In contrast, of the least effective firms, only 21 percent said top managers were bullish on thought leadership (i.e., viewing it as "extremely important" to revenue growth). In fact, an equal percentage said company leaders believe thought leadership is of little or no importance to revenue growth.

But what if you and others in your organization believe it has to make much faster progress with thought leadership? What if competitors have taken mindshare and market share because they created far better content, out-marketed and out-sold your firm, and launched innovative services based on their best-practice thought leadership research?

In my experience, you must generate far stronger buy-in at the top. If you don't, you are not likely to get the resources (time, money and skills) required to accelerate progress. If your firm is in that camp, the next question might be this: "How can we dramatically reduce the time it takes for our top management team to recognize thought leadership as a key capability?"

How do you quickly turn top management from hopeful skeptics of thought leadership to devout advocates? I've seen B2B companies do this in one of three ways:

- Making an inarguable connection between thought leadership and revenue.

- Giving company leaders a taste of what it's like to be seen externally as a thought leader.

- Turning thought leadership R&D into its own profit center (which, of course, ends the complaints about investments with no observable returns).

Each of those actions comes with increasing levels of difficulty, but also increasing levels of returns.

MEASURING THOUGHT LEADERSHIP'S IMPACT IN MONETARY TERMS

First, let's look at metrics that matter to the people who lead companies. CEOs, CFOs, and leaders of practices, regions and divisions understand the language of money: revenue, profit, profit margins, proposals issued, proposals won and other words that have dollar signs attached to them. In contrast, marketers use other metrics to justify their jobs: "quality content," downloads, likes, website visitors and others. Company leaders just don't live in that world.

I say this because it's easy for people like me who are engrossed in the thought leadership profession to forget that while we are fully bought into thought leadership as a revenue driver, people who have never seen it work are not. They don't believe what we believe. As a consequence, we need to talk about the impact of thought leadership in terms that are meaningful to them.

Our survey found the best companies at thought leadership gauge the success of their programs on monetary-related metrics: inbound inquiries, requests for proposals (RFPs), conversions of proposals into project wins and revenue. And, yes, they also are likely to measure content downloads and views. Some measure the dollar value of the work that thought leadership played a role in generating. In contrast, the companies that are weakest at thought leadership typically don't use those measures. Their most common ones are inquiries and content views. Only one out of seven can connect thought leadership to money — i.e., the value of the billable work that it generates.

One of my clients was intent on showing hopeful-but-skeptical management about the value of thought leadership. To illustrate the impact of one of his campaigns, he identified 160 people who attended the firm's conference and more than 350 people, many from Fortune

500 companies, who downloaded the campaign's white paper. Finally, in getting-closer-to-Jerry Maguire language *("Show me the money!")*, he found that 14 of those prospects asked for sales meetings.

An important part of talking to top management about thought leadership is demonstrating that it works — that it has generated revenue and profit. My expertise is *not* in understanding how companies use customer relationship management software such as HubSpot, Salesforce or Marketo to track inquiries from potential clients generated by website content, conference speeches, webinar attendance and other thought leadership activities. I am not an expert in how much a lead (and any revenue that flows from it) can be attributed to thought leadership, client references that a salesperson provided or that salesperson's skills.

But, as the numbers I mentioned earlier show, many B2B companies *do* track the client opportunities generated by their thought leadership investments. Every B2B company that wants to compete on thought leadership must do so — even if top management already buys into it. The reason here is simple: Even when top management doesn't question the thought leadership budget, if the return is a big multiple of the investment, that could suggest the investment is actually too low.

What's more, tracking your thought leadership campaigns will give you insights on which ones are more successful (sometimes far more successful) than others. You will want to understand what accounted for those differences. Was the content superior? If so, how? Was it because the research was more compelling than usual? What led to it becoming more compelling? Was the marketing mix better — e.g., more webinars and seminars than usual? Were salespeople better trained?

In these ways, you want to measure the client revenue impact of thought leadership to (potentially) get a bigger budget than even you thought you deserved, and to improve the way you create, market and sell content. You need those metrics to create a bigger impact.

If you have some thought leadership campaigns, you'll be able to show your company's management what their thought leadership dollars are getting them. That should lead to healthier and more fruitful discussions at budget time.

But if you want to deepen their interest in thought leadership beyond having numbers that are hard to dismiss, my next recommendation will come with a little risk but a lot more upside: showing them what it feels like to be regarded as a thought leader in the marketplace.

GIVING LEADERS A TASTE OF THOUGHT LEADERSHIP

Some of the savviest thought leadership professionals I know realized that getting their internal subject experts famous for their expertise wasn't enough. They also got the CEOs and other company leaders involved, and helped them become recognized as experts in the marketplace.

I look at this as helping a CEO take a test drive with thought leadership — to feel what it's like to be widely recognized for some expertise. Nothing will be more persuasive in making the case for thought leadership than having your CEO watch it work for himself or herself. Getting them recognized as an expert on some topic by getting published in prestigious places and speaking at prestigious conferences, and then personally experiencing the customer inquiries and adulation that great thought leadership produces, is powerful.

Turning the CEO into a thought leader cannot only help companies get religion around thought leadership. It can also give the company a competitive advantage: a CEO who is a highly respected expert leading the company. Two colleagues of mine, John Randolph and John Shannon, and I conducted desk research in 2020 on CEOs who had become recognized as thought leaders since the 1960s, especially on the strength of bestselling books that they authored.[84] We spent three months digging up books by CEOs that positioned them as thought leaders. Our conclusion was that making the CEO a recognized thought leader boosted the fortunes not only of themselves but also their companies. The most prominent examples include GE's Jack Welch, Ogilvy & Mather's David Ogilvy and Satya Nadella of Microsoft.

Along with establishing their reputations as savvy leaders, thought leadership can help CEOs become more respected as forces for social change, which raises the confidence of external and internal stakeholders. In the last few years, CEOs have been weighing in publicly on burning societal issues — racism, the economic impacts of the pandemic, widening income inequality, the environment and more. The reasons for speaking out go beyond just doing the right thing: It could impact their company's financial performance. Consider that 69 percent of more than 11,000 people surveyed in the spring of 2020 said that how CEOs react and communicate on societal topics will "permanently affect their decision to buy from their company."[85]

But in choosing those issues, CEOs and thought leadership heads must consider which stakeholders are most critical at the time — customers, shareholders, employees, acquisition targets or another. A CEO who is considered a thought leader can persuade investors that the firm is in good hands; customers that the firm's expertise is deep at all levels including the top; internal and external talent that the firm is a great place to work; and other stakeholders on issues that make the company more attractive and competitive.

HOW CEO THOUGHT LEADERS CAN BOOST THEIR COMPANY'S BRAND

More than any other executive, CEOs have the greatest ability to get their firms recognized as thought leaders. External and internal audiences put more stock in what a CEO says than they do in any other employee. Why is this the case? When the CEO is an acknowledged expert, outsiders (shareholders, customers, business partners, the media, etc.) may be more likely to assume that the CEO sets the tone for the entire company — i.e., that if the CEO is an expert in a certain area, many other people in the company must be too.

Ogilvy's famous 1963 book, *Confessions of an Advertising Man*, laid out his beliefs about what made great marketing. Ogilvy himself wrote in a subsequent book that *Confessions* helped his ad agency grow from a small "creative boutique" to one of the four biggest agencies worldwide by the mid-1980s.[86] In the 1980s and 1990s, Welch's push to be seen as a management expert helped win over GE shareholders and attract talent. For sure, GE's financial performance was most important in increasing its market value nearly 30-fold to $410 billion.[87] But his stature as a thought leader had to have helped.

Why can the CEO be a company's best thought leader? From our research, we found three primary reasons:

- **The halo effect:** When the CEO is seen as a thought leader in a certain domain, audiences can perceive the entire organizations as having that expertise. When customers view a CEO as a leading expert on how to solve a certain problem, they presume such expertise filters down through the organization. Brand marketers see the halo effect of a strong company brand as creating customer affinity for all its products and services, present and future. Apple, for example, benefits from the halo effect of being a technology and design innovator, especially in the ease with which consumers can use its devices and their elegant design. In companies that sell expertise, a CEO who is perceived to be a leading expert casts a positive light on the entire firm.

- **Media magnetism:** The media covets CEOs' views more than they do any other executives in an organization, given their perch at the top and the difficulty of getting access to them. A study that looked at media coverage from 2010-2012 of 36 Fortune 100 companies correlated the visibility of CEOs with the overall visibility of the companies they ran.[88] In other words, CEOs who make themselves more available to the media also increase the media's coverage of their organizations.

- **The ascender-to-the-throne advantage:** CEOs who didn't launch their companies are perceived as having earned their wisdom from having ascended to the top of an organization. They gained their expertise from knowing how to get employees to collaborate and solve issues. Thus, these CEOs' expertise is seen as coming *not* from academic smarts or research, but rather from their managerial chops — i.e., EQ (emotional quotient or intelligence), not just IQ. For this reason, a CEO's words of wisdom may have a better chance of appearing practical and proven rather than theoretical.

The impact of a CEO who is recognized as a thought leader is not surprising. CEOs occupy the most influential role in their organizations, one whose impact on overall company performance has even been quantified. My co-researchers on this topic and I believe that the companies that would benefit most from a CEO who is regarded as a thought leader either sell expertise for a living (and need to show it to lure more customers) or need to demonstrate deep expertise to win over investors and other shareholders, talent, acquisition targets, suppliers and other business partners, or regulators. We grouped examples by the stakeholders they tried to influence.

Why and On What Companies Should Turn Their CEOs Into Market-Recognized Thought Leaders				
Stakeholder	**Expertise for CEO to Show**	**Reason to Show Expertise**	**Industries of Greatest Need**	**Examples**
Investors & shareholders	Competence in running growing, profitable, value-enhancing firm	Keep firm's valuation high, raise valuation, keep activist investors at bay, keep job	All those with public companies	Jack Welch: Straight from the Gut
Customers	Deep insights on the customer problems that the firm solves, and how to solve them	Firm has deep and superior expertise at all levels, starting at and driven from the top	Professional services, wealth management, research and other firms whose people deliver expertise to customers	Madhavan Ramanujam and Georg Tacke of Simon-Kucher & Partners (Monetizing Innovation)

Why and On What Companies Should Turn Their CEOs Into Market-Recognized Thought Leaders				
Stakeholder	Expertise for CEO to Show	Reason to Show Expertise	Industries of Greatest Need	Examples
Employees	How to create a great workplace (including the workplace the CEO has created)	Talent attraction and retention	High-tech, pharma, research, retail, restaurants, consulting and others facing a "war for talent"	Satya Nadella, CEO of Microsoft: Hit Refresh
Acquisition, investment and funding targets	How to grow acquisitions and startups	Why they should sell to the firm; why they should take investments from the firm	Private equity firms Venture capital firms	Example: David Cote, Goldman Sachs/Vertiv Ben Horowitz, Andreessen Horowitz
Greater public	Firm's recognition of its societal impacts, and how to reduce the negative and increase the positive ones	Influence regulators, voting public, lawmakers and others in power in government (or able to vote them out)	All But especially relevant today for social media, media, food, energy, health insurance and pharma companies	Marc Benioff, co-CEO, Salesforce. com Bill Gates: The Road Ahead (first published in 1995)

Since the 1990s, two CEOs of Simon-Kucher & Partners, today a $400 million revenue global pricing strategy consulting firm, have followed this track. The firm's first CEO to become a recognized thought leader, Hermann Simon (who co-founded the firm in 1985 and led it from 1995-2009) has written more than 35 books, including three during his CEO tenure.[89] In 2016, Simon-Kucher's then co-CEO

Georg Tacke and partner Madhavan Ramanujam published the book *Monetizing Innovation,* which they supplemented with two *Harvard Business Review* articles.[90] Since the book was published, the firm's revenue increased from €240 million to €361 million in 2020.[91,92]

With stories like these, we're surprised that more CEOs of professional services firms, especially the largest of them, have not tried to elevate their credentials as experts. While a number of CEOs and their marketers have attempted this in recent decades, few of these leaders have been recognized as top authorities on their topics. Professors and consultants are more likely to get the kudos.

A biannual ranking of the world's 50 top thought leaders (by the firm Thinkers50) affirms this. Over the last decade, only five CEOs have made their list, by my company's counting. Since 2001, CEOs have occupied only 10 percent of Thinkers 50's 500 slots (10 rankings, 50 slots per ranking). Professors (58 percent) and consultants (21 percent) were chosen far more often.[93]

When the marketplace views a CEO as a thought leader, it can cast a firm's brand image in a stronger light. The internal impact can be equally important: a CEO who, by example, demonstrates to others in an organization why they should strive to be recognized externally for their expertise.

To be sure, some CEOs will use this as a personal PR exercise. They will not encourage or perhaps even permit others in the company to do the same thing. They may feel that sharing the public limelight will dim the light on them. These CEOs won't help their organizations use thought leadership as a competitive strategy. Competing on the basis of organization-wide expertise will stop at the top.

In contrast, CEOs who clear the thought leadership path for others in their organization to follow will be catalysts for strengthening the firm's reputation as problem solvers — if they provide the necessary resources as well as the encouragement. Hermann Simon did that at Simon-Kucher, and the CEOs who have followed him since 2009 did as well. It's what Jim Champy did at CSC Index in the early 1990s. He and Michael Hammer weren't the only "gurus" of reengineering. Other CSC Index leaders became known for applying reengineering principles in different industries and business processes.

Just as Hermann Simon and Jim Champy did, CEOs who propel others down the path of thought leadership will enable deserving employees to show off their organization's expertise at many levels. Like a rowing team where more than one or two people are rowing hard, those companies will gain eminence for their expertise far faster.

After showing a CEO exactly what it's like to be regarded as a thought leader, there's a third way to gain a much stronger embrace of thought leadership at the top of a company.

GETTING CLIENTS TO FUND YOUR THOUGHT LEADERSHIP R&D

The third strategy for accelerating organizational momentum around thought leadership has been used even less frequently than helping CEOs package and market their expertise. However, when executed well, it can have an explosive impact.

It's turning thought leadership research from a cost center to a profit center. It means getting a company's clients and potential clients to fund and participate in research studies that sift out the best practices from the average and worst practices on the topics at hand.

This kind of research is how CSC Index and Hammer developed the blockbuster idea of business reengineering 30+ years ago. It's how the Corporate Executive Board (now part of Gartner) — a company in the thought leadership research business — pioneered a concept for B2B companies called the Challenger Sale. And it is what has powered Dave Ulrich's company, the RBL Group, into an international consulting firm.

Michael Hammer and CSC Index's PRISM research business had about a 10-year run, from the mid-1980s to the mid-1990s, with their research institute for executives running IT at large companies. It began with a single study in the 1980s, commissioned by CIOs to deal with a new technology that their organizations were buying by the hundreds and which they had to support: the IBM personal computer. The PRISM research was the place that Hammer would tell reporters where he "discovered" reengineering. Tom Davenport directed the program on behalf of Index before leaving the firm in 1988. Davenport would write his own classic article on reengineering (for *MIT's Sloan Management Review*) and book.[94]

At its peak, PRISM had more than 100 corporate sponsors, each paying annual membership fees of about $25,000.[95] Hammer and Index shared in the revenue from those sponsorships. The research team (2-4 people in addition to Hammer over those years) studied three to four topics each year that sponsors weighed in on. The quid pro quo of sponsorship was that sponsoring organizations opened up their doors to PRISM research interviewers on each topic. The researchers visited and phoned sponsors in conducting their research interviews. The sponsors provided the case study material to the PRISM researchers — how they and others in their companies were managing and using information technology, and the practices they perceived to be leading to better or worse organizational productivity.

PRISM sponsors would meet with the research team several times a year at a hotel near Index's Cambridge, Massachusetts, headquarters (the Charles Hotel was their favorite) for a couple of days to hear the latest research findings. Many good ideas came out of this research. But the biggest one by far — the blockbuster — was business reengineering.

CSC Index's research partnership with Michael Hammer had borne big fruit by 1990, when the consulting firm began marketing and delivering business reengineering services. The R&D that went into reengineering was paid for by the PRISM sponsors.

But not only had the research sponsors *paid* for the ideas, they were the *source* of those ideas. They were the petri dish in which Mike Hammer and CSC Index's research team observed the practices of Fortune 500 companies that were getting outsized results from IT. Hammer and Index slapped the "reengineering" label on these practices. They marketed the concept through speeches, journal articles (Hammer published a now classic *Harvard Business Review* piece on reengineering in 1990) and books (Hammer and Champy published one of the bestselling business books of the 1990s, *Reengineering the Corporation*, in 1993).

This game has been playing out in similar ways ever since then. The RBL Group was founded in 2000 by Ulrich and Norm Smallwood. They launched the RBL Institute in 2007 as a think tank for people running human resources at large companies around the world. Since then, its membership has reached more than 50 organizations.[96] They, like PRISM's sponsors in the 1980s and 1990s, provide RBL Institute researchers with HR practices to be analyzed and codified into best practices.

What enabled CSC Index and the RBL Group to attract sponsors to underwrite their thought leadership R&D? Two factors were especially important:

- **They were led by charismatic experts with star power and a following.** By the mid-1980s, Michael Hammer had carved out a reputation on the topic of "office automation." He had been a tenured professor of computer science at MIT before jumping into the PRISM research business with Index Group. Hammer had begun to attract a following among senior IT executives. Ulrich had written numerous articles for HR association publications and was rated as a top HR expert by *Business Week, HR Magazine,* and *Executive Excellence.*[97]

- **They were researching emerging, "white-hot" issues with significant white space.** In the late 1980s, most of the research on information technology (by firms like Gartner, Forrester and International Data Corp.) focused on the technology and the companies that developed it. PRISM filled a relatively unfilled void by examining key issues for big buyers of technology: how to manage and use it for competitive advantage. (MIT's Sloan School of Management and other business schools have researched these issues, too.)

It's important to note here the biggest source of value to the firms doing the research — beyond getting someone else to finance the thought leadership R&D. The biggest payoff was developing the intellectual capital the firm needed to bring breakthrough services to market. The value of that far exceeded covering the R&D overhead.

So, as we've seen from some of the best exemplars in this business, getting your firm's leaders — especially the CEO — to become devout advocates of thought leadership is essential. But it may take some convincing. It will require connecting the dots between thought leadership and revenue, giving leaders a taste of the adulation that comes with being recognized as a thought leader and maybe even turning thought leadership R&D into a profit center.

But even after your leaders have been convinced of the transformative power of thought leadership, your work is not done. You'll need to turbocharge your capabilities — and avoid falling into traps that can derail even the best intentions. The final chapter explores these momentum boosters and busters.

CHAPTER 11

ACCELERATING THE MOMENTUM

+   +   +   +   +   +   +   +

A s you come to this last chapter in the book, and if you haven't skipped ahead to get here, you have read how to develop and codify compelling ideas; how to create big demand for those ideas; and how to scale up services based on the ideas.

That is, you've learned what it takes to compete on thought leadership.

I hope you now see that it's not just a marketing activity to be done alongside brand and product marketing. It's not just publishing bestselling books or groundbreaking articles in prestigious journals. It's not just a way for salespeople to do consultative selling.

Rather, competing on thought leadership is a firm's strategy to out-think, out-market and out-deliver expertise that solves its clients' problems. It's about accelerating revenue and profit by developing superior expertise, getting target clients to embrace it and delivering it at a level of quality that competitors can't match.

As you can imagine, that's a tall order. But a number of companies have shown over the last 50 years that it *is* possible to do.

This decade, many more companies will try to compete on the basis of thought leadership. From our research and client experience, I believe the race will be faster and more competitive.

We've seen this change in our own client base and in the types of people who've inquired about our services. In the late 1990s they were almost exclusively management consulting firms; over the last decade we've added clients in software, IT services, architecture, real estate management, public policy think tanks, pharmaceuticals and medical devices, wealth management, law, accounting, and training and development.

We've also seen increased thought leadership budgets through the surveys that we have done over the years. In our 2020 survey of more than 300 B2B companies, the average budget for thought leadership was 5.5 percent of revenue — and a tenth of them spend 10 percent of their revenue or more on it.

More people are choosing thought leadership as a career. The number of people on LinkedIn who have the words "thought leadership" in their job titles or responsibilities has grown to nearly 500,000 as of this writing. We've seen specialist firms focusing on thought leadership for lawyers, tech companies, healthcare firms, and many other professions and industries.

We look at these and other indicators as signposts that thought leadership, as a strategy and as a profession, is ascending. But whether it ascends or descends in a company is a different matter. In this final chapter, I'll leave you with thoughts on how your firm can make it ascend, and guard against its descent. I talk about this in terms of thought leadership momentum boosters and busters.

First, the momentum boosters.

BOOSTERS OF THOUGHT LEADERSHIP

Five momentum boosters are of greatest importance: a top-down push for innovative new services; advanced case research skills; finely honed capabilities in argument development; a high-quality flagship journal; and a steady supply of present and upcoming gurus. Let's look at each one.

A Penchant at the Top for Service Innovation

Thought leadership at its finest is about service innovation. It's about bringing R&D practices that have long been differentiators in manufacturing to firms that sell expertise billed by the hour. The culture set at the top of CSC Index was one of innovation. Its R&D with Michael Hammer changed the operations consulting industry forever.

For thought leadership R&D to lead to new services or new practices for existing services, it must be encouraged at the very top of the company. If it isn't, a B2B firm's existing service lines are likely to resist the new services or new practices that come out of thought leadership R&D.

Accenture, a $44 billion professional services company, has a strong focus on driving change through insight. Francis Hintermann is the global managing director of Accenture Research, leading a team of 300 researchers based in 20 countries around the world. Working with guidance from the global leadership team, Hintermann has positioned Accenture Research as a driver of new approaches for new and existing practices and services.

When firms are resistant to service innovation, they sequester thought leadership R&D as a marketing activity — not as new service and practice development initiatives. At such firms, thought leadership means only creating demand but not supply.

Advanced Case Research Capabilities

When thought-leadership-fueled service innovation is part of a B2B firm's culture, it should be no surprise that the second momentum booster lies in R&D: the ability to understand what differentiates a set of organizations that are among the best at addressing a particular business problem from those that are among the worst.

The ability to do extensive case study research and gain new and crucial insights from it is a big momentum booster of thought leadership. The more extensive the research, and the better its research teams can collectively "connect the dots" about why the best are indeed the best, the greater advantage a company has to compete on thought leadership.

More extensive case research means conducting more and deeper interviews with companies dealing with the topic at hand. It means interviewing several dozen companies, not a handful, on a topic. Deeper is about interviewing multiple people at each company, not just one, to get several views on how their firm is handling an issue. Each person interviewed brings a different perspective; typically, no one person in a firm fully understands why it is leading or trailing on some matter.

People's ability to articulate these issues can also vary significantly. In many case interviews I've conducted, I've often found that only one person in a firm has both unique insights and exceptional explanatory skills in discussing how the organization addressed some issue.

While nothing replaces interviewing people in firms that are on both ends of the "success" spectrum and at points in between, additional research also adds to the richness of the insights. Far more material can be found on the web today than in the early 1990s, when case research was possible only if companies were willing to be interviewed. Company blogs, speeches on YouTube and Vimeo, transcripts of quarterly financial analyst calls at public companies, archived press articles — all of these give the thought leadership case researcher many more places to pan for gold.

The Ability to Find and Develop Talented Argument Shapers

Companies must have stellar skills not just in case study research but also in thought leadership marketing campaign management, methodology development, training and development, thought leadership selling, data visualization, and more. However, since the largest source of regular thought leadership content will be a firm's client experiences, another skill stands out as crucial here: argument shaping.

I explained what argument shaping was in Chapter 5. It's much harder to find a great argument shaper than a great writer. Thus, companies that know where to recruit and how to develop argument shapers will have a content edge. I believe this is a skill that in most cases will need to be developed, given the low supply of talented argument shapers that I see.

But be sure your argument shapers come with the right motivation and passions. Ex-journalists will need to be okay with losing the byline and being the "ghost" to company experts whose arguments they push. Ex-lawyers can't want to win every debate with your company's thought leaders (or aspiring ones) on how to craft the argument, as they would in preparing for a trial. And ex-researchers could resent helping company experts gather facts and sharing credit for connecting the dots. All your argument-shaping people must have a passion for letting others in the company make money from the ideas they help develop.

A Fabulous Flagship Thought Leadership Journal

Dozens of B2B firms have these publications: McKinsey, PwC (through its 2013 acquisition of Booz & Company), Accenture, Tata Consultancy Services, Cognizant, Roland Berger, Gensler and FTI Consulting, to name just a few examples.

A regular thought leadership journal is a staple of the thought leadership marketing mix, even if "regular" means once a year. Having compelling content for that journal is a requirement, too. That requires editors who are highly skilled at helping company professionals shape and communicate powerful arguments.

Why must companies that compete on thought leadership have a flagship journal that regularly conveys their thoughts? I see three reasons:

- **Brand establishment:** As a tangible and continual signal that the firm wants to be recognized for its expertise.

- **Content quality control:** Through having professional editors who enforce content standards for articles.

- **Intellectual purity:** By having a regular publication that provides wisdom rather than peddles services.

Producing an exceptional thought leadership journal requires a commitment at the top of a company, and not just a commitment of money. The executives who run a B2B firm must ensure their journal doesn't turn from an educational tool into a blatant promoter of the company's offerings. They also must contribute their expertise in articles, and encourage the firm's brightest to contribute theirs, too.

Gurus, Present and Future

Clients not only want to work with *firms* that possess superior expertise; they also want to work with the *people* in those firms who have the specific knowledge they need. This is why one of the goals of thought leadership must be not only to burnish your firm's reputation for its expertise, but also your people's reputation.

Firms that compete on thought leadership must market themselves differently than firms that don't need to compete this way. Consider the automobile industry: Do BMW, Mercedes or Lexus drivers buy these cars because they were designed by some premiere car designer whose name they know and respect? I doubt it. Haven't Apple customers continued to buy iPhones and Apple Watches and other products long after the 2011 passing of co-founder Steve Jobs and the 2019 exit of its famed design chief Jony Ive? Or did your company purchase a Salesforce software license because founder and now co-CEO Marc Benioff — or someone else — was the mind behind the design of the system? Not likely.

In contrast, clients are attracted to firms and people in those firms who are thought leaders because they are buying expertise — thoughts turned into services. The more people in a B2B firm who are recognized for their expertise — seen as gurus in their niches — the better it is for that firm.

But people who earn guru status also can become demanding once they achieve it. Companies such as Bain have kept many of their thought leaders from bolting. Others don't. Ultimately, only by creating a pipeline stocked with up-and-coming gurus can a firm reduce the odds that its heavy investments in turning several experts into gurus will vaporize when they leave.

The five strategies I just mentioned will help turbocharge thought leadership at your firm. But it won't make you immune from very common problems that can undermine it or kill it altogether. Be aware of momentum busters like the ones below.

AVOID THE BUSTERS

I've seen many momentum busters over the years. But few have been as destructive as the following three.

Brand and Product Marketing Creep

Every company needs to project and protect a strong brand image. Apple's brand is about making technology elegant and easy to use. Disney's brand is about wholesome family entertainment. Goldman Sachs' brand is about elite deal-making skills in acquisitions and divestitures, and in new public stock offerings and other financing that public companies need. Mercedes' brand is about elegance in automobiles, and the BMW brand is about performance in those luxury cars. Toyota's is about reliability and quality.

Product marketing executives spend their professional lives getting consumers to recognize the strengths of their company's offerings vs. those of the competition.

But when brand and product marketing executives are brought in to run marketing at firms that sell expertise, they often can — as one would expect — see thought leadership as another set of marketing programs that should be run like brand and product marketing programs. Thought leadership journals start running articles that brag too much about the firm's services or feature customer testimonials that are a bit too glowing. In-depth research studies that used to weigh in at 100 pages or more are reduced to sound bites — five-to-10-page highlight reports that no longer present in-depth thinking.

Or thought leadership journals, books, op-ed submissions, public speaking presentations and other "high-bandwidth, low-bias" marketing forms are put on the shelf altogether. In their place go the low-bandwidth, high-bias marketing channels of advertising, trade show booths and brochures.

Thought Leadership R&D Reporting to Marketing

If a brand or product marketer doesn't take control of thought leadership marketing, a chief marketing officer who's a big proponent of thought leadership can swoop in and seek to control the thought leadership R&D function. This is problematic on two fronts.

The first is that any hope of thought leadership research turning into new services, or new practices in existing services, is likely to go by the wayside. The reason is that the rest of the company, seeing thought leadership R&D reporting to marketing, will view the content as something for the marketers.

The second problem I've seen is CMOs who shrink the R&D budget in favor of the marketing budget. The best companies at thought leadership spend considerable sums on R&D and don't let marketing control that budget.

Not Ensuring Intellectual Credit and Recognition

This is a big pet peeve and an insidious practice: when people write or contribute substantial thought to articles and studies but their names don't show up in the credits. I understand why some B2B firms do this: They have junior associates collect research and volunteer ideas that will make it into partners' articles. Or they have working professionals — consultants, lawyers, accountants, etc. — who contribute their expertise to thought leadership content but reserve the bylines for the people who will sell or lead the work.

If you want to discourage future potential thought leaders in your firm from contributing their ideas, you couldn't find a better way to do it than this. It is not only dishonest, but also bad business if your firm wishes to compete on thought leadership.

Creating a culture of thought leadership requires giving people in a firm the best incentive for contributing their thoughts — intellectual credit for original and compelling ideas.

A GOLDEN AGE FOR THOUGHT LEADERSHIP

+   +   +   +   +   +   +   +

A S YOU FINISH THIS book, I hope you now share my excitement about the power of thought leadership to change the basis of competition, and the opportunities in this emerging profession.

By the end of the decade, I hope to be writing about a field that has blossomed and become fully recognized for its importance and its opportunities. I believe thought leadership has the potential to become a glamorous field, just like advertising and media. In fact, I see thought leadership disrupting the field of B2B advertising, much as streaming services have disrupted how we consume entertainment.

Here's why I think this way. With the rise of internet-distributed movies and other entertainment programs, it would be no exaggeration to call the last decade the Golden Age of Streaming. It is changing the paradigm of how movies, television shows, plays and concerts are produced and presented, and disrupting the advertising model that once underpinned them. Between 2016 and 2020, streaming companies' global revenue increased nearly threefold, to $62 billion. The number of original series produced for U.S. streaming services rose by a factor of four (from 131 to 537).[98] Streaming series such as "The Crown," "Schitt's Creek" and "Ozark" are not likely to fade soon from our memories.

I predict a similar golden age this decade for business-to-business companies that compete on the basis of thought leadership. Their hits will be the latest versions of business reengineering, disruptive innovation, emotional intelligence and customer loyalty management. And like the streaming entertainment, they will reach their markets in a totally new way that will shift paradigms and short-circuit the old marketing methods.

But I also predict that one of the greatest casualties from effective thought leadership marketing will be the "brand journalism" and "advertorials" we see today in major publications, which are seeking new sources of revenue by offering pay-for-play. Special advertising sections with glowing articles about companies, written in a journalistic style, will become far less credible. Genuine thought leadership will replace advertorials. Companies whose innovations and brilliant ideas earn the attention of real journalists will ultimately have the winning hand. Getting through those gatekeepers at major news outlets will be critical.

With strong processes and people who can conduct case study research and create groundbreaking ideas, package and market those ideas in compelling ways, and develop quality services at scale, companies that grow on the back of thought leadership will have a distinct competitive advantage. And if they have the momentum boosters firmly in place and consciously avoid the momentum busters, little can stop them from keeping that advantage.

How can I be so bullish on thought leadership? Why don't I believe that thought leadership — just like the many management concepts created by thought leaders that have lost their pizzazz — too will lose its luster?

I am not basing my prediction on sophisticated scenario planning exercises. Nor have any soothsayers at large or small professional services firms whispered this in my ear. I have only anecdotes and factoids behind my optimism, although they are in line with the three forces discussed in Chapter 2 that have generated great demand for genuine expertise in recent decades.

For example, the COVID-19 crisis provides the perfect example of customer complexity. To formulate and distribute global vaccines to fight this scourge, pharmaceutical companies and health care providers had to run global clinical trials; manufacture and distribute vaccines worldwide simultaneously; and tackle the enormous headaches of getting vaccines into people's arms. This was the global healthcare industry's equivalent of a moon shot, but it happened … to the world's collective joy, amidst a terrible and continuing loss of human life before vaccines arrived. The healthcare and pharmaceutical industries could not have pulled off this moon shot without relying on the expertise of thought leaders outside their industries — in the consulting, legal, political, project management, regulatory, technology and other realms. If you believe the world will be subject to more pandemics this decade, you would have to believe that demand for additional expertise in dealing with them will, too, be robust.

I also wrote about the complexities that digital technologies were inducing in organizations everywhere in recent decades. Are those complexities likely to subside this decade? Not likely, in a world of accelerating technology breakthroughs and change. Consulting firms like McKinsey have been bringing proprietary technology to the table in recent years — not just the proprietary thinking of their consultants. For example, in early 2021 it launched an analytics software platform to help clients improve the overall experience that they provide *their* customers. McKinsey called its platform a "significant leap toward real-time, comprehensive customer insights," saying it cuts the time for the average company to take action on customer surveys from about a month to a moment.[99]

Consulting firms becoming data analytics providers — just like software behemoths SAS Institute, Oracle and SAP? McKinsey wouldn't be doing this unless it felt its clients needed more than just advice to improve their customer experiences.

The third complexity I discussed in Chapter 2 — competition coming from new places — should also be expected to increase this decade. Consider global advertising agencies and their advice to their clients (advertisers) on where to put their ads. Prior to the year 2000, that discussion was largely about how to allocate spending in TV, radio, print, billboard and other marketing channels. Now that digital advertising channels have overtaken non-digital ad channels, the decision is more about whether to advertise with Amazon, Facebook, Google or another digital company.

Who's to say some new social media network might not gain fast ground this decade and become a big ad target? Or Netflix, with its 200 million in global subscribers?[100] You can bet that advertisers will need advice from their ad agencies about which marketing channels to use, and when, and how to optimize their messages. The need for new expertise in how to capitalize on digital marketing channels — especially those (like Amazon and Walmart.com) that can provide not only viewer demographics but also purchasing statistics — will be in big demand.

Your clients and customers are going to need *new* expertise to deal with these rising complexities. You're going to have to develop that expertise, and package, market and sell it. Your firm will have to deliver that expertise at scale when more clients clamor for it.

The opportunities for companies that know how to compete on thought leadership will be vast. But competitors will emerge with the same ambition as yours: to be seen as *the* leading expert in their fields, which of course are also your fields.

This is what will make thought leadership an even more exciting and more lucrative profession. The number of business problems for companies to solve for the rest of this decade will be endless. The firms with the best expertise will win big. So will the people who can help their firms develop, become recognized for and deliver that expertise.

ACKNOWLEDGMENTS

+   +   +   +   +   +   +   +

MY APOLOGIES FOR APPROPRIATING the African proverb, but it does take a village to build a career in thought leadership. A college degree doesn't give you the skills to help others gain widespread recognition for their expertise (at least not yet). Even after your first experience developing a bestselling book or publishing a groundbreaking article in a prestigious journal, I argue that you haven't "made it" yet. Your journey towards mastery of this profession must continue.

And if you decide to leave the comfortable corporate environment, selling thought leadership skills to the marketplace requires another set of capabilities. Those skills are about running a firm, keeping clients coming back, and making the work stimulating and worthwhile for the people who do it.

You can't learn this all by yourself. You need people who inspire you, challenge you, provide breaks and believe in you throughout your journey. With that in mind, I wrote this acknowledgements section not only to thank people who've helped me over the years, but also to encourage readers to find similar allies as they grow in this profession.

My thought leadership village since 1987, the year I entered the profession, has included a special group of advisers, business partners, colleagues, bosses, clients, and affiliates.

ON LAUNCHING MY THOUGHT LEADERSHIP CAREER

The first person to bring center stage is Tom Waite. Tom made thought leadership an attractive profession when I was a business journalist. He hired me away from CMP Publications in 1987 to work at his then-small marketing department at Index Group. (That firm's head of HR, Pauline Johnson, must also get a mention, for convincing Tom that I would be a wise hire.) Tom later became the firm's chief marketing officer, a few years after its acquisition by Computer Sciences Corp. in 1988 (thus the rebrand of CSC Index). Importantly, he smoothed out my rough journalist edges — which included an off-putting, probing reportorial style — and showed me how to work effectively with sharp consultants. Thank you so much Tom, for starting and sending my thought leadership career in the right direction. (Tom also has demonstrated how thought leadership professionals can climb to even higher altitudes, having published five novels since 2012.)

If you're contemplating a career in thought leadership, I hope your first boss is a Tom Waite.

HOW TO DO THOUGHT LEADERSHIP RESEARCH RIGHT

My first close look at thought leadership R&D was getting a peek inside the PRISM research program that birthed the blockbuster management concept of the 1990s: business reengineering. When I joined Index in 1987, I asked Tom if I could attend the PRISM conferences, a business that was co-owned by Michael Hammer and CSC Index. Mike was a profound thinker and magnetic speaker on business technology issues. Talking to Mike was what I imagined talking with Einstein to be like: You knew you were in the presence of superior intellect.

Mike had a great team of researchers and research directors in PRISM, including Thomas H. Davenport, who left in 1988 to carve out an illustrious career as a business technology guru at McKinsey, Accenture, Ernst & Young, and several universities (including Babson College).[101] For the last 30 years, Tom has been a leading voice on the business utility of analytics, enterprise systems, knowledge management, artificial intelligence, and business process redesign. I learned lots from Bob Morison, Sarah Kaull, Brad Power, Susan Rubin, the late Susan Cohen and others were researchers on the PRISM team during the glory years of reengineering.

Mike also had dozens of loyal and riveted research sponsors. He was the veritable straw that stirred the drink. At the start my career in thought leadership, he and Tom Davenport showed me, and many others, where path-breaking, thought-leading ideas come from: after taking significant time to think about what you learned from in-depth interviews of dozens of companies (and multiple executives in each company) and divining how the best at solving the business problem at hand differed from the worst. They left an indelible impression on how thought leadership research should be done.

Tom is still going strong at the thought leadership game. Tragically, Mike died way too young, at age of 60 in 2008, leaving behind a loving family, numerous colleagues and thousands of ardent fans of his research on how information technology can dramatically change the way companies operate.

Starting my thought leadership career at CSC Index while Mike and Tom Davenport were there was like landing that first post-college job to promote an up-and-coming Liverpool band called the Beatles. You attend some sessions and beer hall concerts, and sense something big is about to happen. When it does, you have to pinch yourself that you have a ringside seat to a blockbuster concept and the opportunity to promote it.

During my time at CSC Index I learned much from other outstanding thought leadership R&D professionals: Jim Wetherbe (a professor at Texas Tech University), former Harvard Business School Dean Nitin Nohria (when he was an associate professor), UC Irvine Prof. Vijay Gurbaxani, Nick Vitalari, Chunka Mui and Michael Treacy.

Dave Ulrich, Liz Wiseman and Shane Cragun gave me valuable input on how to turn thought leadership into services. All are recognized thought leaders in their domains.

I hope you have the chance to work with thought leaders like these.

I have also learned lots from other thought leadership research professionals over the years, especially from Serge Perignon of Tata Consultancy Services, Ajit Kambil of Deloitte's CFO program, and Francis Hintermann of Accenture Research. And Binayak Choudhury and his colleagues at Phronesis Partners have been great teachers for me on designing survey research.

All the folks in this section are all-stars in the arcane field of bringing new research-based insights to life.

ON HOW TO CREATE DEMAND WITH THOUGHT LEADERSHIP

As I've explained in this book, great ideas don't necessarily command the audience they deserve. Marketing and selling services that implement those ideas is elemental, too, to compete on thought leadership. I've had a multitude of marketing and business development mentors here: Tom Waite, of course, but also the late Ron Christman, John Shannon, John Randolph and their colleagues at CSC Index who worked in its extensive research and advisory business. No one knew better than Ron how to weave together thought leadership and recreation for executives attending resort-based events.

Since the late 1980s numerous *Harvard Business Review* editors have taught me what's required to get into the world's leading management publication. I want to thank everyone I've known, pitched to and worked with there, starting with Geraldine Willigan (who went on to help make Ram Charan famous with his books). Geri has been a trusted confidante for 30+ years. My dear friend Ellen Peebles (with whom I worked at CSC Index, and who went on to work at HBR) was also a great teacher. Like Mike Hammer, Ellen passed away way too early, and I am just one of many who miss her warmth, wit and humor. Other HBR mentors (current and former) include Sarah Green Carmichael (now at Bloomberg Opinion), Sarah Cliffe, Eben Harrell, Jeff Kehoe, Julia Kirby, Dan McGinn, Gardiner Morse, Steve Prokesch, Tom Stewart and Nicole Torres. Cathy Olofson, once of Harvard Business Review Publishing and more recently chief marketing officer of consultancy Innosight, has also given me excellent insights into working with HBR over the years. She has also been a speaker at conferences that I have co-sponsored. Thank you, Cathy, for your valuable insights and friendship.

Frederick Allen, the longtime editorial lead of *Forbes*' Leadership Section, has been a great teacher on how to get opinion articles and columnists' writings accepted at this influential business publication. Now retired, Fred and *Forbes* have shown the good things that happen when business publications provide platforms for outside experts. Thank you, Fred, for your wisdom and guidance in helping several of my clients become *Forbes* contributors over the last decade.

These editors have taught me numerous lessons about how to get big and fervent audiences for thought leaders. Marketers need to build strong and productive relationships with editors, even if they reject some of your pitches. (I know what that's about!) They are your gatekeepers to big audiences who need to know about your firm's expertise. Transactional relationships are not likely to get you through their gates with the frequency you need. Get to know them, and what they need, extremely well. They have careers to maintain, just like you.

Since writing and argument development are a key part of thought leadership marketing, I encourage you to learn from other writers too. Over the years I have worked with gifted writers who humbled me with their capabilities and motivated me to write better myself: David Rosenbaum, Mike Goldberg, David Case, Kate Sweetman, Laurianne McLaughlin, the late Pat Wright, and many others.

ON HOW TO BE A VALUED PARTNER TO CLIENTS

My clients over the years have taught me, and continue to teach me, how to get better at my game. I can't name them all (this book does need to end at some point!), and I apologize to ones I don't mention here. My first shout-out goes to TCS and its Thought Leadership Institute, especially Serge Perignon, who runs it, and his colleagues Suzanne Rose, Derek Baker and Laura Rudolph, as well as the firm's many digital experts whose expertise we have tapped. A big thank you as well to Krishnan Ramanujam, the TCS executive who has been championing its thought leadership research activities and the *Perspectives* management journal over the last decade.

Other highly valued clients (present and past) include the Richard M. Schulze Family Foundation (which launched and supports the Entrepreneurship & Innovation Exchange academic journal that we edit, working with Jim Wetherbe, David Deeds and other professors); FMG Leading (Richard Aldersea, Matt Brubaker, Steve Cokkinias, Foster Mobley, and Jennifer Perry, among others); Robert Sher of Mastering Midsized; Hank Cardello (formerly at the Hudson Institute, now at Georgetown University's Leadership Solutions for Health and Prosperity Program); Madhavan Ramanujam and Georg Tacke (Simon-Kucher & Partners); and Roger Jones (founder of The Trusted Advisor Project). And I have been the beneficiary of deep knowledge on diversity and inclusion from clients Karen Brown of Bridge Arrow, and Angela Vallot and Mitchell Karp of VallotKarp. This year, Todd Warner and James Fulton have introduced me to a whole new take on corporate culture.

Over the last decade, I have learned tons from thought leaders, thought leadership researchers and marketers from such companies as Cognizant (where Alan Alper has been a stellar thought leadership pro), Leader Networks (the incomparable Vanessa DiMauro), The Moery Company (led by the inspirational J.P. Moery), Kido Communications (led by PR maven Veronica Kido), Authentic Identity (Tony Tiernan, a whiz at helping professional firms establish brands that resonate), Deloitte, CSC, Accenture, EY and Marakon Associates. And I hold a special place in my heart for Sara Noble, thought leadership recruiter nonpareil, whose counsel and vast network of editorial whizzes have helped numerous elite organizations turn their ideas into compelling insights.

My learning curve has been steep and exhilarating since 1998, when Bernie Thiel and I launched our first thought leadership consultancy. By the way — thank you Bernie and Susan Buddenbaum (who later became a Bloom Group partner) for a great 10-year run.

Whether your clients — current and aspiring thought leaders — are inside or outside your firm, you need to learn how to work effectively with them. When egos bruise easily, this can be very difficult. Nonetheless, *your* ultimate success will be measured by *their* ultimate success in the crowded marketplace of substantive ideas. When you remind them that you're on their side, trying to help them have market impact, it can defuse even the tensest moments.

ON HOW TO RUN A CONSULTING AND MARKETING FIRM

Within a company it's common to have disagreements with colleagues about how to manage the business and the future direction of the firm. I've experienced this myself. Allies from outside the business can provide perspective and a reality check.

The "Profiting from Thought Leadership" conference that my previous firm and Rattleback launched in 2016 showed me the importance of events in my own thought leadership marketing mix. For that conference, and for several surveys on thought leadership, I thank Jason Mlicki, Rattleback's chief, for a great alliance. Jason has been a terrific partner on the events and research fronts.

Alliance partners like Rattleback are essential. But so are company advisers. In forming Buday TLP in 2020, I felt I needed advisers who are close to, but not inside, this firm to keep me honest. In that regard, I am extremely fortunate to draw on the guidance of Jim Wetherbe, Richard Aldersea and Robert Sher. They believe in the value of this book as much as I do. Funny thing: I've been telling aspiring thought leaders that the pinnacle of their success comes *after* they write a good book. After too many years, I finally took that advice myself. Thank you, Jim, Richard and Rob, for reminding me to take my own medicine.

And speaking of the book, thanks to the people who provided valuable early input on my first draft, including Tom Buday (my brother, who retired this year from his job as Nestle's global head of marketing and consumer communication), Alan Alper, Robert Sher, Jim Wetherbe and Richard Aldersea.

With alliance partners and advisers like these, thought leadership professionals who wish to make a business in this field will have wind behind their sails.

ON WHAT'S MOST IMPORTANT

The most important people in my village are Catherine Buday and our children: Rachel Mansour, Jesse Buday, Rachel Flynn, Benjamin Buday, Ryan Flynn, and John Buday. My spouse, partner in life and co-worker at Buday Thought Leadership Partners, Cathy is the person who made this book possible. After too many years in which I let other demands get in the way at the previous firm that I co-owned (Bloom Group), she urged me to clear the decks after I launched Buday TLP in 2020 and write this book.

A former journalist and now a Buday TLP principal, writer/editor and web- and newsletter master, Cathy strongly encouraged me to codify what I've learned in this profession, after my several aborted attempts to write a book since 2010. She is the primary editor of this book.

Cathy has shown me what's most important. It's not a book, or a career, or money. It's having a life partner who elevates the happiness and well-being of everyone around them.

ENDNOTES

Prologue

1 Gartner data, according to a Dec. 16, 1996, *New York Times* article by Glenn Rifkin, "Re-engineering Firm Tries Some of Its Own Medicine." *https://www.nytimes.com/1996/12/16/business/re-engineering-firm-tries-some-of-its-own-medicine.html*

2 *Reengineering the Corporation*, by Michael Hammer and James Champy (1993). *https://www.amazon.com/Reengineering-Corporation-Manifesto-Revolution-Essentials/dp/0060559535*

3 Thomas A. Stewart, "Reengineering: The hot new managing tool," *Fortune*, Aug. 23, 1993. *https://money.cnn.com/magazines/fortune/fortune_archive/1993/08/23/78237/index.htm*

4 Michael Hammer, "Reengineering Work: Don't Automate, Obliterate," *Harvard Business Review*, July-August 1990. *https://hbr.org/1990/07/reengineering-work-dont-automate-obliterate*

5 *Computerworld*, Jan. 10, 1994.

6 Alex Markels, "Champy Joins Perot Systems To Lead Consulting Efforts," *The Wall Street Journal*, Aug. 20, 1996. *https://www.wsj.com/articles/SB840496593248024000*

7 David Stout, "A Best-Seller Plot Is Said to Be Charged," *The New York Times*, July 27, 1995. *https://www.nytimes.com/1995/07/27/books/a-best-seller-plot-is-said-to-be-charged.html*

Chapter 1

8 Alphabet Inc. press release on 2020 earnings, published Feb. 2, 2021. Alphabet is the parent company of Google. https://abc.xyz/investor/static/pdf/2020Q4_alphabet_earnings_release.pdf?cache=9e991fd

9 Max Lewontin, "Why a US court agrees Google Books is a 'card catalog for the digital age," *The Christian Science Monitor*, Oct. 20, 2015. *https://www.csmonitor.com/Technology/2015/1020/Why-a-US-court-agrees-Google-Books-is-a-card-catalog-for-the-digital-age*

10 Google explanation of its nGram viewer tool. *https://books.google.com/ngrams/info*

11 Porter Anderson, "NPD: 'A Decade of Personal Exploration' Ahead in US Self-Help Books," Publishing Perspectives, Jan. 17, 2020. *https://publishingperspectives. com/2020/01/npd-sees-decade-of-personal-exploration-opening-usa-self-help-books/*

12 Robert Buday, Bernie Thiel, Susan Buddenbaum, and Tim Parker, "Thoughts on Thought Leadership: Insights on Creating Demand for Professional Services," published in 2008. This was a compilation of Bloom Group's articles published from 1998 to 2008. *https://www.amazon.com/Thoughts-Leadership-Insights-Creating-Professional-Services/dp/0615224164*

13 Ceri Parker, "The World Economic Forum at 50: A Timeline of Highlights from Davos and Beyond." Dec. 20, 2019. *https://www.weforum.org/agenda/2019/12/ world-economic-forum-davos-at-50-history-a-timeline-of-highlights/*

14 Christopher Alessi, "Who's Coming to Davos 2020, and Everything Else You Need to Know" Jan. 17, 2020. *https://www.weforum.org/agenda/2020/01/davos-2020-who-is-coming-and-everything-you-need-to-know/*

15 Benjamin Wallace, "Those Fabulous Confabs," *New York*, Feb. 24, 2012. *https:// nymag.com/news/features/ted-conferences-2012-3/*

16 American Express interview with Wurman in 2014. *https://www.americanexpress. com/en-us/business/trends-and-insights/articles/richard-saul-wurman-teds-founder-discusses-how-it-all-began/*

17 Emma Grey Ellis, "The Oral History of TED, a Club for the Rich That Became a Global Phenomenon," *Wired*, April 28, 2017. *https://www.wired.com/2017/04/an-oral-history-of-ted-talks/*

18 Benjamin Wallace, "Those Fabulous Confabs," *New York*, Feb. 24, 2012. *https:// nymag.com/news/features/ted-conferences-2012-3/*

19 TED web page. *https://www.ted.com/about/our-organization/history-of-ted*

20 Esther Snippe, "TED: The banned talks and what we can learn from them," SpeakerHub, Aug. 15, 2019. *https://speakerhub.com/skillcamp/ted-banned-talks-and-what-we-can-learn-them*

21 Business Insider 2017 profile on TED, *https://www.businessinsider.com/ted-talks-company-profile-2017-10*

22 Wikipedia page on Jorn Barger. *https://en.wikipedia.org/wiki/Jorn_Barger*

23 Growth Badger. *https://growthbadger.com/blog-stats/*

24 Margit Wennmaachers, "Doubling Down on the Future." *https://a16z. com/2021/01/25/doubling-down-marketing-update-new-media/*

25 Quora post by an a16z managing partner, Scott Kupor. *https://www.quora.com/ Why-is-Andreessen-Horowitzs-URL-a16z-com*

26 Axios article, published Feb. 9, 2021. *https://www.axios.com/wordpress-vip-parsely-publishing-e35db863-1970-4420-ad89-fa0ff26d7732.html?utm_campaign=organic&utm_medium=socialshare&utm_source=email*

27 LinkedIn page, *https://business.linkedin.com/marketing-solutions/blog/linkedin-b2b-marketing/2021/why-you-should-be-marketing-on-linkedin-right-now*

28 Fidelity Investment webpage, *https://www.fidelity.com/bin-public/060_www_fidelity_com/documents/about-fidelity/Fidelity_Investments_2020_AnnualReportInfographic.pdf*

29 Aptiv PLC earnings press release, Feb. 3, 2021. *https://www.aptiv.com/en/newsroom/article/aptiv-reports-record-fourth-quarter-financial-results*

Chapter 2

30 Innosight research, "Corporate Longevity: Turbulence Ahead for Large Organizations." *https://www.innosight.com/insight/creative-destruction/*

31 Strategy &/PwC report. *https://www.strategyand.pwc.com/gx/en/insights/ceo-success.html*

32 Spencer Stuart and *The Wall Street Journal*: *https://www.spencerstuart.com/research-and-insight/chief-marketing-officer-average-tenure-drops-to-43-months https://www.wsj.com/articles/average-tenure-of-cmos-falls-again-11590573600*

33 Pew Research/Journalism.org. *https://www.journalism.org/fact-sheet/newspapers/*

34 Michael Barthel, Katerina Ava Matsa and Kirsten Worden, "Coronavirus-Driven Downturn Hits Newspapers Hard as TV News Thrives," Pew Research Center, Oct. 29, 2020. *https://www.journalism.org/2020/10/29/coronavirus-driven-downturn-hits-newspapers-hard-as-tv-news-thrives/*

35 David Shepardson, "Internet sector contributes $2.1 trillion to U.S. economy: industry group," Reuters, Sept. 26, 2019. *https://www.reuters.com/article/us-usa-internet-economy/internet-sector-contributes-2-1-trillion-to-u-s-economy-industry-group-idUSKBN1WB2QB*

36 U.S. Bureau of Economic Analysis. *https://www.bea.gov/system/files/2020-08/New-Digital-Economy-Estimates-August-2020.pdf*

37 Ocean Tomo statistics as cited in article by Ben Carlson, "How tech stocks 'ate' the stock market," *Fortune*, Jan. 21, 2021. *https://fortune.com/2021/01/21/stock-market-tech-stocks-companies-gdp-employees-us-workers-data-charts/*

38 John Huey, "America's Most Successful Merchant," *Fortune*, Sept. 23, 1991. *https://money.cnn.com/magazines/fortune/fortune_archive/1991/09/23/75513/index.htm*

39 U.S. Army Heritage & Education Center. *https://usawc.libanswers.com/faq/84869*

40 See the review section of Glassdoor.com. *www.glassdoor.com*

41 "Why B2B Sellers Need a Sense Making Sales Strategy," Smarter With Gartner, Aug. 20, 2019. *https://www.gartner.com/smarterwithgartner/b2b-sellers-need-sense-making-sales-strategy/*

42 University Research Corridor Profile: James Anderson. *https://urcmich.org/urc-profiles/james-anderson/*

43 Dun & Bradstreet number. *https://www.dnb.com/business-directory/company-profiles.urban_science_applications_inc.442a9833ea48be6a1dbbcf0f01df0db2.html*

44 Urban Science's employee count is based on its LinkedIn company profile. https://www.linkedin.com/company/urban-science

45 Internet Association. *https://internetassociation.org/publications/measuring-us-internet-sector-2019/*

46 Reuters. *https://www.reuters.com/article/us-usa-internet-economy/internet-sector-contributes-2-1-trillion-to-u-s-economy-industry-group-idUSKBN1WB2QB*

47 "8 Top Findings in Gartner CMO Spend Survey 2018-19," Gartner, Nov. 5, 2018. *https://www.gartner.com/en/marketing/insights/articles/8-top-findings-in-gartner-cmo-spend-survey-2018-19*

48 "Four reasons Netflix should expand into video games," *The Conversation*, March 13, 2020. *https://theconversation.com/four-reasons-netflix-should-expand-into-video-games-133464*

49 I developed this model in the late 1990 with Tom Waite and Allan Cohen when they were running Waite & Company.

Chapter 3

50 Ford's ad budget was estimated to be $2.3 billion in 2019 by *Advertising Age* magazine. "Leading National Advertisers Fact Pack." *https://s3-prod.adage.com/s3fs-public/2020-07/lnafp_aa_20200713_locked.pdf*

51 "Crucial Yet Burdened: Thought Leadership Marketing in the Pandemic," Profiting from Thought Leadership study, published February 2021. *https://budaytlp.com/2020/12/17/crucial-yet-burdened-thought-leadership-marketing-in-the-pandemic/*

52 Jeanne Thompson presentation at the 2018 "Profiting from Thought Leadership" conference. https://www.thoughtleadershipseminar.com/?people=jeanne-thompson

53 From a presentation by Jill Kramer and Francis Hintermann at "Profiting from Thought Leadership," Nov. 17, 2020.

Chapter 4

54 Jim Collins' website. *https://www.jimcollins.com/books/research.html*

55 From an email exchange with Dave Ulrich on March 23, 2021.

56 Jennifer Perry, Foster Mobley and Matt Brubaker, "Most Doctors Have Little or No Management Training, and That's a Problem," *Harvard Business Review*, Dec. 15,

2017. *https://hbr.org/2017/12/most-doctors-have-little-or-no-management-training-and-thats-a-problem*

57   This graphic is from FMG Leading's foundational point of view document, "Turning Great Doctors Into Great Leaders," by Jennifer Perry, Foster Mobley, and Matt Brubaker, Sept. 5, 2017. *https://www.fmgleading.com/insights/turning-great-doctors-into-great-leaders*

58   Beverly Kaye, Cile Johnson and Lynn Cowart, "Keeping the Talent You Need Most," published in 2017. *https://talent-dimensions.com/about/white-paper/*

Chapter 5

59   *Hindustan Times* (2010 market cap for TCS), article dated Oct. 22, 2020, *https://www.hindustantimes.com/analysis/the-india-moment-in-the-100-billion-club/story-pmoISN0hYhanvOijLDkCpJ.html*. In January 2021, it reached $169 billion, according to *BusinessWorld*. http://www.businessworld.in/article/TCS-Once-Again-Becomes-The-Most-Valued-Domestic-Firm-By-Market-Capitalisation/25-01-2021-369828/.

60   BuzzSumo and Mantis Research 2018 survey of 700 marketers. https://mantisresearch.com/state-of-original-research-for-marketing-in-2018/

61   Jordan Mintzer, "Francis Ford Coppola Offers Advice to Budding Filmakers at the Lumiere Festival," *The Hollywood Reporter*, Oct. 19, 2019. *https://www.hollywoodreporter.com/news/general-news/francis-ford-coppola-offers-advice-budding-filmmakers-at-lumi-festival-1248870/*

Chapter 6

62   Madhavan Ramanujam and Georg Tacke, "Monetizing Innovation: How Smart Companies Design the Product Around the Price" (Wiley, 2016). My firm at the time, Bloom Group, helped the authors (partners at Simon-Kucher) turn their ideas into manuscript prose. https://www.simon-kucher.com/en-us/resources/books/monetizing-innovation

63   *HBR's* unsolicited article acceptance rate in the 2010s, from my conversations with two former editors.

64   Amanda H. Goodall, *Social Science & Medicines*, "Physician-leaders and hospital performance: Is there an association?" August 2011. *http://ftp.iza.org/dp5830.pdf*

65   Jennifer Perry, Dr. Foster Mobley, and Dr. Matt Brubaker, "Turning Great Doctors Into Great Leaders," FMG Leading, published September 2017. *https://www.fmgleading.com/insights/turning-great-doctors-into-great-leaders*

Chapter 7

66 Full credit for these terms goes to strategy and marketing consultant Allan Cohen, whom I worked with when he was at Waite & Company.

67 Statista. https://www.statista.com/statistics/265796/us-search-engines-ranked-by-number-of-core-searches/

68 According to a 2020 report by We Are Social and HootSuite. https://wearesocial.com/blog/2020/01/digital-2020-3-8-billion-people-use-social-media

69 Cale Guthrie Weissman, "How Emailing 'I Love You' Translated Into $1 Million In Data Analysis Revenue," *Fast Company*, June 20, 2016. *https://www.fastcompany.com/3061344/how-emailing-i-love-you-translated-to-1-million-in-data-analysis-revenue*

70 Tenzin Pema, "Anand Sanwal on building CB Insights via a B2B newsletter that gets a lot of love from data and technology enthusiasts," YourStory, Sept. 7, 2020. *https://yourstory.com/2020/07/anand-sanwal-cb-insights-b2b-newsletter-data-startups-technology*

71 Julie Segal, "Ray Dalio's Brand Power," *Institutional Investor*, Oct. 9, 2019. *https://www.institutionalinvestor.com/article/b1hhqh6x4hj9r3/Ray-Dalio-s-Brand-Power*

72 Angelo Calvello, "Ray Dalio's Book Has Sold a Million Copies. But Who's Actually Implementing His Ideas?" Institutional Investor, May 10, 2018. *https://www.institutionalinvestor.com/article/b184ggn6dd6090/ray-dalio's-book-has-sold-a-million-copies-but-who's-actually-implementing-his-ide.*

73 Ray Dalio's Twitter, LinkedIn and Facebook pages, visited June 21, 2021.

Chapter 8

74 "Email timeline,"*The Guardian*, March 13, 2002. *https://www.theguardian.com/technology/2002/mar/13/internetnews*

75 Edmund Lee, "The New York Times Tops 7.8 Million Subscribers as Growth Slows," *The New York Times*, May 5, 2021. *https://www.nytimes.com/2021/05/05/business/media/nyt-new-york-times-earnings-q1-2021.html?searchResultPosition=1*

76 Nick Bartzokas, Mika Grondahl, et al., *The New York Times*, "Why Opening Windows Is a Key to Reopening Schools," Feb. 26, 2021. *https://www.nytimes.com/interactive/2021/02/26/science/reopen-schools-safety-ventilation.html*

Chapter 9

77 Glenn Rifkin, "Re-engineering Firm Tries Some of Its Own Medicine," *The New York Times*, Dec. 16, 1996. *https://www.nytimes.com/1996/12/16/business/re-engineering-firm-tries-some-of-its-own-medicine.html*

78 From a March 4, 2021 Zoom call with Liz Wiseman.

79 March 18, 2021 phone call with Shane Cragun.

80 Whole Brain Thinking is a product of Herrmann Global LLC. *https://www. thinkherrmann.com/how-it-works*

81 Email exchange with Dave Ulrich, March 24, 2021.

82 According to the firm's chief marketing officer, Tom Waite, during the firm's heady reengineering years. Phone call with Waite on March 6, 2021.

83 Dave Ulrich, Rensis Likert Professor, Ross School of Business, University of Michigan, and partner, The RBL Group. Working paper "Making Knowledge Productive: Suggestions from and for a Personal Journey."

Chapter 10

84 Buday TLP white paper, "When CEOs Need to be Seen as Thought Leaders (and When They Don't)," 2020. *https://budaytlp.com/2020/07/25/when-ceos-need-to-be-seen-as-thought-leaders-and-when-they-dont/*

85 Victoria Sakal, "Bigger Than The Boardroom: Evolving Expectations of Today's CEOs," Morning Consult, June 10, 2020. *https://morningconsult.com/2020/06/10/bigger-than-the-boardroom-evolving-expectations-of-todays-ceos/*

86 David Ogilvy, *Ogilvy on Advertising*, published by Vintage Books, 1985. *https://www.amazon.com/Ogilvy-Advertising-David/dp/039472903X*

87 Chris Noon, "Jack Welch, the 'Ultimate Manager' who Oversaw GE's Rise to the Most Valuable Company, Dies at 84," March 2, 2020. *https://www.ge.com/news/reports/jack-welch-the-ultimate-manager-who-oversaw-ges-rise-to-the-most-valuable-company-dies-at-84*

88 Nicole Lee, PRIME Research, "The Relationship between CEO Media Coverage and Overall Organization Media Coverage," Institute for Public Relations, 2012. *https://www.instituteforpr.org/wp-content/uploads/Lee_IPR_CEOs.pdf*

89 HermannSimon.com biography. *https://hermannsimon.com/cv/*

90 My colleagues and I at my previous firm (Bloom Group) helped Simon-Kucher produce *Monetizing Innovation.*

91 Simon-Kucher press release, Jan. 27, 2021. *https://www.simon-kucher.com/en/about/media-center/simon-kucher-steady-growth-path*

92 Consultancy.eu, with chart on Simon-Kucher's revenue growth since the year 2000. *https://www.consultancy.eu/news/3964/simon-kucher-books-10th-consecutive-year-of-growth*

93 Thinkers50 Ranking on *https://thinkers50.com/t50-ranking/*

94 Thomas H. Davenport, "Business Process Reengineering: Where It's Been, Where It's Going," paper, p. 18. *https://ebpm.ir/wp-content/uploads/2017/10/Business-Process-Change-_-Reengineering-Concepts-Methods-and-Technologies-1998.pdf*

95 From a July 2021 discussion with John Shannon, who sold sponsorships for PRISM and other CSC Index research services.

96 RBL Institute video, June 2019, on YouTube . *https://www.youtube.com/watch?v=3JoZdc-5A5I*

97 Dave Ulrich bio on the RBL website. *https://www.rbl.net/about-us/consultants/dave-ulrich*

Epilogue

98 Motion Pictures Association, 2020 Theme Report. *https://www.motionpictures.org/wp-content/uploads/2021/03/MPA-2020-THEME-Report.pdf*

99 McKinsey press release, Jan. 25, 2021. *https://www.mckinsey.com/business-functions/marketing-and-sales/solutions/periscope/news/press-releases/mckinsey-and-company-revolutionizes-customer-experience-with-experience-dna-launch*

100 Jessica Toonkel, "Banished by Netflix, Advertising Makes Comeback on New Streaming Services," The Information, March 10, 2021. *https://www.theinformation.com/articles/banished-by-netflix-advertising-makes-comeback-on-new-streaming-services*

Acknowledgments

101 To get an overview of Tom Davenport's star-filled career as a thought leader on issues at the intersection of business and information technology, see the "About" page on his website. https://www.tomdavenport.com/about/

INDEX

Page numbers in **bold** denote non-textual matter.